BAPTIST DISHES WORTH BLESSING

Library - South Wing   Joy Rust

Baptist Dishes Worth Blessing

EDITED
by
JUDY BRYSON

ILLUSTRATED BY
JOY RUST

PELICAN PUBLISHING COMPANY
GRETNA 1978

Cookbook Committee

Mrs. Harold Bryson, Chairman

Mrs. Ronald D. Albright
Mrs. Chris Barbee
Mrs. Jerry Barlow
Mrs. Clay Corvin
Mrs. Paul E. Earley
Mrs. Carroll B. Freeman
Mrs. Bill Hanks
Miss Kathryn Harper
Miss Martha Haynie
Mrs. Tony Hendrix
Mrs. Clayton Jordan
Mrs. Tommy Kinchen
Mrs. Russell McIntire
Mrs. Carl McLemore
Mrs. Mike McLemore
Mrs. Tommy Mills
Mrs. Paul Robertson
Mrs. Ray Rust
Mrs. Hugh Tobias
Mrs. Timothy R. Williams

Library of Congress Cataloging in Publication Data

Main entry under title:

Baptist dishes worth blessing.

Includes index.
1. Cookery, American. I. New Orleans. Baptist Theological Seminary.
TX715.B235   641.5   78-631
ISBN 0-88289-188-X

Manufactured in the United States of America

Published by Pelican Publishing Company, Inc.
630 Burmaster Street, Gretna, Louisiana 70053
Typesetting by New Hampshire Composition, Concord, New Hampshire

Contents

Foreword

Hospitality is a grand old Southern custom, and for most of us at New Orleans Baptist Theological Seminary, it is a way of life. Webster defines the word *hospitable* as the quality of "being entertaining, or fond of entertaining, guests in a friendly, generous manner." This attitude is nothing new to Christians, because in Romans 12:13 we are told to "get into the habit of inviting guests home for dinner or, if they need lodging, for the night." In Peter 4:9 we are told: "Cheerfully share your home with those who need a meal or a place to stay for the night." This cookbook is the result of our belief that hospitality is a characteristic of all followers of Jesus Christ.

From the beginning, our purpose has been threefold: first, to provide some help in the form of menus, recipes, and suggestions for our student wives going out to perform literally a "ministry of hospitality"; second, to have a project in which students, alumni, and faculty could simultaneously be involved; third, to provide a source of revenue for undergirding the cost of physical improvements on campus.

We are indebted to scores of people for their help in tackling the many details involved in this project. Joy Rust, in particular, has added immeasurably with her beautiful sketches of our campus. Thank you one and all.

Jo Ann Leavell

Look In the Bible

WHEN

Anxious for loved ones—Psalms 121; Luke 17
Fortune declines—Psalms 37, 92; Ecclesiastes 5
Downhearted—Psalms 23, 42, 43
Things go wrong—II Timothy 3; Hebrews 13
Friends seem to let you down—Matthew 5; I Corinthians 13
In grief—Psalms 46; Matthew 28
In temptation—Psalms 15, 19, 139
Depressed—Psalms 34, 71; Isaiah 40
Busyness—Ecclesiastes 3:1-15
Sleepless—Psalms 4, 56, 130
Disagreeing—Matthew 18; Ephesians 4; James 4
Exhausted—Psalms 95:1-7; Matthew 11
Worried—Psalms 46; Matthew 6

IF YOU

Are challenged—Ephesians 6; Philippians 4
Are confronted with a crisis—Job 28:12-28; Proverbs 8; Isaiah 55
Are envious—Psalms 49; James 3
Are confronted with impatience—Psalms 40, 90; Hebrews 12
Are saddened by loss of a loved one—1 Corinthians 15; I Thessalonians 4:13-5:28; Revelation 21, 22
Are wearied by boredom—II Kings 5; Job 38; Psalms 103, 104; Ephesians 3

WHEN

Wanting inward peace—John 14; Romans 8
In prosperity—Psalms 33:12-22, 100; I Timothy 6; James 2:1-17
Self-satisfied—Proverbs 11; Luke 16
Concerned about business—Matthew 7
Beginning new employment—Psalms 1; Proverbs 16; Philippians 3:7-21
Placed in a responsible position—Joshua 1:1-9; Proverbs 2; II Corinthians 8:1-15

Establishing a home—Psalms 127; Proverbs 17; Ephesians 5; Colossians 3; I Peter 3:1-17; I John 4
Desiring harmony with fellowmen—Romans 12

TO FIND

The Ten Commandments—Exodus 20; Deuteronomy 5
The Shepherd Psalm—Psalms 23
The Birth of Jesus—Matthew 1, 2; Luke 2
The Beatitudes—Matthew 5:1-12
The Lord's Prayer—Matthew 6:5-15; Luke 11:1-13
The Sermon on the Mount—Matthew 5, 6, 7
The Great Commandments—Matthew 22:34-40
The Great Commission—Matthew 28:16-20
The Good Samaritan—Luke 10
The Prodigal Son—Luke 15
The Sower—Matthew 13; Mark 4; Luke 8
The Last Judgment—Matthew 25
The Crucifixion, Death, and Resurrection of Jesus—Matthew 26, 27, 28; Mark 14, 15, 16; Luke 22, 23, 24; John 13-21
The Outpouring of the Holy Spirit—Acts 2

IF YOU

Are filled with hate—Luke 6; II Corinthians 4; Ephesians 4
Have suffered losses—Colossians 1; I Peter 1
Have disobeyed God—Isaiah 6; Mark 12; Luke 5
Have sinned—Matthew 23; Luke 15; Phelemon
Are physically ill—Psalms 6, 39, 41, 67; Isaiah 26

WHEN YOU

Falter in your faith—Psalms 126, 146; Hebrews 11
Feel remote from God—Psalms 25, 125, 138; Luke 10
Are absent from home—Psalms 119; Proverbs 3, 4
Are making financial plans—Mark 4; Luke 19
Wane in strength—Matthew 25; Revelation 3
Are lonesome and afraid—Psalms 27, 91; Luke 8: I Peter 4
Are fearful of dying—John 11, 17, 20; II Corinthians 5; I John 3; Revelation 14
Are worshiping God—Psalms 24, 84, 116; Isaiah 1:10-20; John 4:1-45
Feel love of country—Deuteronomy 8; Psalms 85, 118, 124; Isaiah 41:8-20; Micah 4, 6:6-16

History of New Orleans Baptist Theological Seminary

The New Orleans Baptist Theological Seminary was voted into being in 1917 by the Southern Baptist Convention meeting in New Orleans. Christened the Baptist Bible Institute, a name it bore until 1946, the seminary was the first theological institution that the Southern Baptist Convention, as such, created. In so doing, a century-old dream of Baptists in the South became a reality.

It was in 1817 that Cornelius Paulding had first proposed the establishment of such a school in southern Louisiana, a region then viewed as the gateway to Latin America.

Later, in 1849, Dr. Basil Manly, Sr., had referred to the location of an institution for the training of preachers and missionaries in New Orleans as "very rational, feasible, and eligible." In the 1890s, Dr. J. B. Gambrell had actually conducted three successive, annual Pastors Theological Institutes in the First Baptist Church of New Orleans. Again and again that project came into the purview of religious statesmen because of the need for a ministerial training institution in the Deep South and because of the unique opportunities of missionary endeavor and experience in southern Louisiana.

Dr. P. I. Lipsey reopened the subject vigorously in 1914 by his editorial in Mississippi's *Baptist Record*. Three subsequent years of planning culminated in the action of the Southern Baptist Convention in session at New Orleans in 1917, whereby the Home Mission Board and Sunday School Board were instructed to cooperate with the Mississippi and Louisiana State Conventions in establishing a theological school. The school held its first session in October, 1918, under the leadership of Dr. Byron Hoover DeMent. In 1925, ownership and control were formally assumed by the Southern Baptist Convention.

Because of ill health, Dr. DeMent resigned as president on

December 1, 1927. He continued as professor of New Testament, however, until his death, March 17, 1933. On January 25, 1928, Dr. Duke Kimbrough McCall, then pastor of Broadway Baptist Church, Louisville, Kentucky, was elected president. He served until May 1, 1946, at which time he became executive secretary of the Executive Committee of the Southern Baptist Convention. On May 14, 1946, the Trustees elected Dr. Roland Quinche Leavell as president. Dr. Leavell was then pastor of the First Baptist Church, Tampa, Florida.

In 1957 Dr. Leavell suffered an illness that forced his retirement. During an interim period of one year, Dr. James Washington Watts served as acting president. Dr. H. Leo Eddleman, president of Georgetown College in Kentucky, was elected president on November 25, 1958, and assumed his duties on February 1, 1959. Dr. Eddleman resigned effective February 28, 1970, and Dr. James D. Mosteller was appointed acting president. Dr. Grady C. Cothen, who at the time was president of Oklahoma Baptist University, was elected president of New Orleans Baptist Theological Seminary on September 17, 1970. He served until March 1, 1974, when he resigned to become president of the Sunday School Board of the Southern Baptist Convention. Dr. Ray P. Rust completed the year as acting president. Dr. Landrum P. Leavell II, pastor of the First Baptist Church of Wichita Falls, Texas, was elected president on December 10, 1974.

The rich traditions and vibrant cultural atmosphere of New Orleans are a part of the life of the seminary. From its beginnings in 1918, until 1953, the seminary was located at 1220 Washington Avenue, in the heart of the Garden District of residential New Orleans. The seminary had been purchased in 1918 from the H. Sophie Newcomb College. Its history reaches back into the 1850s, however, when the buildings and grounds belonged to the site of a magnificent private mansion.

Land for a new campus was purchased in 1947, and construction on the first buildings began in 1948. Approximately 7 million dollars have been invested in new facilities since that time.

Formal dedicatory exercises were conducted on September 3, 1953. The seminary now has a campus that is both beautiful and functional.

Menus

Graduation Open House at the President's Home

Pineapple Refresher (p. 22)
Mocha Punch (p. 24)
Sausage and Cheese Balls (p. 32)
Cheese Straws (p. 31-32)
Sand Tarts (p. 41)
Shrimp Sandwich Spread (p. 34)
Cinnamon Bars
Cook-While-You-Sleep Cookies (p. 170-71)

Christmas Open House

Martha Washington Candy
Party Strawberries (p. 39)
Frozen Fruit Cookies
Lemon Squares (p. 40)
Cocktail Wieners (p. 35)
Hot Seafood and Shells or Melba Toast (p. 28-29)
Shrimp Dip (p. 31)
Hot Spiced Percolator Punch (p. 23)
Seminar Punch (p. 20)
–The Committee

Bridal Tea

Coffee
Tricolored Ices (p. 147)
Cheese Straws (p. 31-32)
Pecan Meringues (p. 40)
Butter Cookies (p. 167)
Parsley Wheel Sandwiches (p. 35)
–Mrs. Fred Mosley

New-Faculty Luncheon

Orange Cooler (p. 22)
Fresh Broccoli and Cauliflower with Dip
Cheese Soufflé (p. 72)
Shrimp Mold with Crisp Vegetables and Sour Cream (p. 105)
Dilly Bread (p. 131)
Easy Crepes with Strawberry Sauce (p. 139-40)

Freeze some juice in an ice tray. Put frozen cubes in Orange Cooler to keep juice cold while guests are arriving.

Place crushed ice in a large wooden bowl. Arrange chilled Fresh Broccoli and cauliflower rosettes on ice.

Dip: Mix one envelope Ranch-style salad dressing mix with Sour Cream. Put in a small bowl and put in center of ice and vegetables.

Put lettuce on large silver tray in the center of Shrimp Mold. Surround mold with crisp carrots, olives, and tomato wedges.

Sour-Cream Sauce: Dice two cucumbers, drain, and add to sour cream. Salt to taste. Serve with mold.

–Mrs. Harold Bryson

New-Member Luncheon Salad

(Serves 20)

5 heads Lettuce
5 Tomatoes, diced
6 Cucumbers, cut with skin (rounds not strips)
5 Green Peppers, cut
1 stalk Celery, cut
1 package Carrots, grated
2 jars Olives (drained)
3 bunches Little Green Onions, cut with tops
1 jar sliced Dill Pickles (drained)
3 cans diced or sliced Beets (drained)
3 jars Bacon Bits (crushed)
2 pounds Cheddar Cheese (grated fine)
3 loaves French Bread
2 cans Sardines or Anchovies (optional)
1 quart Blue Cheese or Roquefort Dressing
1 quart French Dressing
2 quarts Thousand Island Dressing
1 Quart Oil and Vinegar
Croutons

For croutons, cut loaf of bread in small squares and bake in 250° oven for approximately 2 hours or until very dry and crisp.

Put all ingredients in separate containers. Use ice tongs for everything except croutons, olives, and bacon bits.

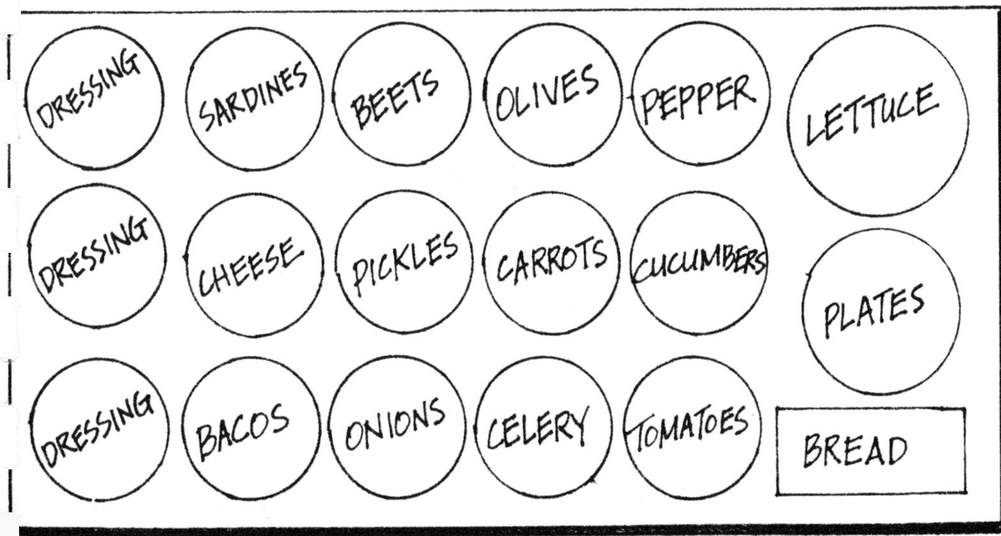

Let everyone "create" his own salad. The more ingredients you add, the better! Try the beets and cheese, and you'll be hooked.

–Eastdale Baptist Church, Montgomery, Alabama

NOTE: This is a monthly meeting at the church to get acquainted with new members. A nursery is provided also.

Refreshments for a Club Meeting

Hot Shrimp Dip (p. 30)
Pecan Tassies (p. 39) Cheese Niblets (p. 33-34)
Apricot-Coconut Balls (p. 37)
Coconut Loaf Cake (p. 38) Chocolate Surprise (p. 39)
Hot Spiced Tea (p. 23) Punch
Coffee
–Mrs. W. L. Stagg, Jr. (Lula), Pineville, Arkansas

Ladies' Luncheon

Theme: Quilting Bee
Decor: Patchwork tablecloths and napkins made from sheets of patchwork pattern
Invitation: Written on patchwork wrapping or notepaper
Centerpiece: Wire basket or straw basket lined with patchwork material and filled with flowers (formal) or eggs (informal)

Menu
Curried Chicken Cups (p. 87-88)
Fruit Salad with Poppyseed Dressing (p. 66)
Refrigerator Bran Muffins (p. 129)
Hot Spiced Tea (p. 23)
Strawberry Passion Dessert
–Mrs. Tom Monroe

Sunday Brunch

Eggs Benedict (p. 69)
Melon Balls
Sweet Rolls (p. 133)
Coffee and Juice
–Mrs. Bill Rogers

Bridal Luncheon

Sandwich Loaf (p. 134)
Carrot Curls and Black Olives
Chips
Chocolate Ice-Box Dessert (p. 142)
–Mrs. Bill Rogers

Meatless Meal Luncheon

Fresh Spinach Salad (p. 64)
Quiche Lorraine (p. 70-71)
Broccoli with Butter
Ice Cream on Chocolate Almond Pie (p. 158)
–Mrs. Ray Rust

Sunday Dinner

Chilled V-8 Juice with Parsley Sprig
Tossed Salad
Broiled Chicken Breast with Apple Rings
Carrot-Ring Platter (p. 115)
Rolls Butter Jelly
Angel Food Cake with Sherbet
–Mrs. H. Leo Eddleman

Dinner for Four

Chicken Curry (p. 80)
Broccoli Delight (p. 111)
Mandarin Orange Salad
Gougère (p. 132-33)
Blueberry Cream Fluff (p. 142)
–Mrs. David Odom

Deacons and Wives Dinner

Broccoli and Chicken Casserole (p. 88)
Baked Apricots (p. 61)
Green Layer Salad (p. 64)
Homemade Bread (p. 128)
Holiday Ice Cream (p. 146)
–Mrs. James Richardson

Dinner for Six

Chicken Parmesan (p. 85)
Broccoli-Rice Casserole (p. 111)
Frosted Fruit Salad (p. 55)
Hot Rolls (p. 127)
Ice Cream Balls with Chocolate Sauce (p. 146)
–Mrs. Bill Rogers

Mexican Dinner

Guacamole Salad (p. 62)
Easy Enchiladas (p. 90)
Tacos (p. 99)
–Mrs. Leroy Yarbrough

Beverages

Are you preparing beverages for a crowd? Here are some ways to make your task easier.

Coffee: One pound of coffee plus 2 gallons of water equals 40 cups of coffee.

Tea: For hot or cold tea, make tea concentrate ahead of time. *Tea concentrate*: Bring to a boil 1½ quarts of fresh cold water. Remove from heat and add ¼ pound loose tea leaves. Stir, cover, and let brew for 4 minutes. Strain into teapot or jar and cover lightly. This mixture can be stored at room temperature for several hours. It makes enough concentrate for 40-45 cups of hot tea or 30-35 glasses of iced tea. *Serving cold drinks*: A cold beverage is best served in a chilled glass or cup. (In this volume a PUNCH CUP is a 4-ounce serving; a REGULAR CUP is 8 ounces. When serving fruit drinks or punch, figure on 4 ounces of beverage per serving.)

To fancy up your ice cubes for punches, freeze fresh berries, mint leaves, or lemon or orange slices in ice trays; freeze fruit juice or add food coloring to water; or, add small pieces of fruit or vegetable (depending on the drink) into trays filled with water or beverage.

To prevent the flavor of your punches from weakening, use ice cubes frozen from the juice of your beverage instead of from water.

To frost glasses with a flourish, dip the edge of a glass first in lemon or orange juice, then into a mound of granulated sugar. Chill in the refrigerator or freezer.

A variety of punches can be frozen and then defrosted just in time to have slivers of icy beverage left in them.

Ginger ale has two noteworthy advantages as a punch ingredient: (1) it is easily enhanced—a few squirts of fruit juice will do

Frost Building

the trick—and (2) it can be used to extend a punch recipe if a crowd should happen to exceed your expectations.

Garnishing cold drinks: Fruit slices such as lemons, limes, and oranges are great as finishing touches for punch bowls or individual drinks. Pull a lemon stripper over the rind of a fruit at uniform intervals to remove the peel in thin strips; then slice the fruit crosswise.

Mint leaves can be used to garnish drinks. Cloves can be used both to season and garnish. Puncture orange slices with whole cloves, then float the slices in your beverages. Decorative touches: Instead of using a block of ice to chill a punch bowl, use frozen fresh fruit. Nectarines, peaches, cherries, grapes, and whole pineapple all freeze well.

In the summertime, large fresh leaves taken from your garden and placed under beverage glasses make a drink look tropical and refreshing. Similarly, glasses will look inviting if placed rim down in a huge watermelon filled with crushed ice. They will also stay frosted and cool without any extra trouble.

Ice rings: To prepare a frozen ring in which fruit, mint leaves, flowers, and so on, are suspended, first freeze a ring ⅓ full of water. Add the desired garnish or decoration and increase the water to ⅔ full. Freeze again. Then completely fill the ring with water and freeze for the last time.

FROZEN BANANA PUNCH (Serves 32)

2 pkg. strawberry Kool-Aid
2 qt. water
2 bananas, mashed
2 c. sugar
juice of 2 lemons
1 (46 oz.) can pineapple juice

Mix all ingredients well and freeze. Makes gallon. Remove from freezer an hour or so before ready to serve. Serve as a slush.

–Mrs. Billy K. Smith (Irlene)

LIME PUNCH (Serves 32)

1 pkg. lime jello
4 c. hot water
1 large can frozen lemonade
2 c. sugar
1 large can (unsweetened) pineapple juice
1 qt. ginger ale

Mix lime jello and hot water until jello is dissolved. Add sugar, pineapple juice, and lemonade. (All this may be done ahead of time and mixture refrigerated.) Just before serving, add ginger ale and ½ gallon lime sherbet if desired.

–Mrs. Melvin J. Poole (Linda)

PUNCH FOR 150

Dissolve jello in boiling water. Add sugar to solution and bring to boil once more. Mix all ingredients except ginger ale. Add the cold water and chill. Make an ice ring of some of the punch. When ready to serve, add the ginger ale or Sprite for sparkle.

–Mrs. W. L. Stagg, Jr. (Lula)

6 pkg. jello
4 c. boiling water
12 c. sugar
3 (46 oz.) cans pineapple juice
2 small bottles almond flavoring
3 small cans frozen lemon juice
1 gal. cold water
5 large bottles chilled ginger ale or Sprite

SEMINARY PUNCH (Serves 48)

Mix all ingredients well. The afternoon before serving, place in freezer. Stir frequently as punch starts to freeze. Serve directly from freezer; it will be mushy and does not require ice.

–The Committee

1 (46 oz.) can orange juice
1 (46 oz.) can pineapple juice
1 medium bottle lemon juice
1 pkg. lemon-lime Kool-Aid, unsweetened
6 c. water
2 c. sugar

LEMON-STRAWBERRY PUNCH (Serves 28)

In a large punch bowl, prepare lemonade as directed on can; stir in strawberries (with syrup). Stir in ginger ale, and if you wish, add small scoops of ice cream (various flavors for color effect) or colored ice cubes.

–Mrs. Paul Earley (Jackie)

3 (6 oz.) cans frozen lemonade
1 qt. ginger ale, chilled
1 (10 oz.) pkg. frozen strawberries, thawed

FRUIT PUNCH (Serves 30)

Mix lemonade and orange juice as directed on the can. Add juices to punch bowl. Put soda water in at last minute. Decorate with sprigs of mint and orange and lemon slices. Chill.

–Mrs. "Skip" Archer (Catherine)

1 large can frozen lemonade
1 small can frozen orange juice
1 (46 oz.) can pineapple juice
1 bottle soda water

WILLIAMSBURG FRUIT PUNCH (Serves 64)

Mix all ingredients and chill. Add ginger ale before serving.

–Mrs. William P. Tuck (Emily)

2 qt. strong tea
4 c. orange juice
1½ qt. cranberry juice
2 c. lemon juice
2 c. sugar
2 qt. water
1 qt. ginger ale

WEDDING PUNCH (Serves 100)

Prepare orange juice as directed. Mix all ingredients except sherbet in a large bowl. Scoop sherbet into punch and serve.

2 (6 oz.) cans frozen orange juice
2 qt. Hawaiian punch
2 qt. pineapple juice
1 can fruit cocktail
4 qt. water
lime sherbet

ORANGE PUNCH (Serves 150)

Boil the sugar with the 3 pints of water. Dissolve the jello in the 12 cups of hot water and add to the sugar mixture. Add all of the juices. Just before serving, add the flavoring and ginger ale. (Some people like more ginger ale than others.)

–Maurine Austin Dudley

12 c. sugar
3 pt. water
6 pkg. orange and lemon jello
12 c. hot water
3 large cans frozen orange juice
3 large cans frozen pineapple juice
3 large cans frozen lemon juice
1 medium bottle almond flavoring
2 or more qt. ginger ale

EASY MAKE-AHEAD PUNCH (Serves 25)

Mix the above well and pour into a plastic gallon milk jug. Then add water, but do not fill the jug to the top. Freeze to a slush. When ready to serve, cut off top of jug and the slushy mix will come out easily. At serving time, add the ginger ale. For added flair, freeze a ring mold of punch mix and use in bowl instead of ice cubes—mixture will not get watered down. TIP: If you make this several days in advance of a party or want to keep some on hand, freeze and then take out several hours before serving. You want the punch mixture to be slushy when you put it into the punch bowl. Multiply the recipe as many times as needed.

–Mrs. John F. Gibson

2 small pkg. unsweetened Kool-Aid (for improved flavor, mix reds as 1 strawberry and 1 cherry or 1 cherry and 1 raspberry)
2 c. sugar
½ tall can pineapple juice
1 qt. ginger ale

PINEAPPLE REFRESHER PUNCH (Serves 40)

1 (46 oz.) can orange-pineapple juice
1 (46 oz.) can pineapple juice
½ gal. pineapple sherbet
1 small can crushed pineapple (optional)
2 qt. ginger ale

Freeze the orange-pineapple and pineapple juice. Remove from freezer long enough to make slush. Put slush in punch bowl. Add pineapple sherbet, crushed pineapple, and ginger ale. NOTE: To change color of punch, substitute orange-pineapple juice with red Hawaiian punch and raspberry sherbet. To make a green punch, substitute lime jello for pineapple.

This recipe was found on the kitchen cabinet of the seminary president's home.

–Mrs. Landrum P. Leavell (Jo Ann)

ORANGE COOLER

1 part orange juice, chilled
2 parts Sprite, chilled

Mix and chill. Serve. *–The Committee*

ORANGE JULIUS (Serves 6)

½ c. frozen orange juice
½ c. sugar
½ t. vanilla
½ c. milk
½ c. water
5-6 ice cubes

Combine all ingredients in a blender; cover and blend until smooth, about 30 seconds. Serve immediately. *–The Committee*

TROPICAL ICE (Serves 6)

1 can crushed pineapple
2 c. orange juice
Dash of salt
2 c. mashed bananas
½ doz. maraschino cherries
1 T. lemon juice

Mix all of the above. Freeze. To make less solid texture, beat after partially frozen and freeze again. NOTE: May be used as dessert, on lettuce and with mayonnaise as salad, or in ginger ale for punch.

–Mrs. John Pedersen (Murfi)

TASTY SHAKE (Serves 6)

1 pt. vanilla ice cream
2 c. milk
2 eggs
1 (16 oz.) can peaches

Blend above ingredients in blender for 30 seconds. Strawberry, cherry, or any other equal amount of fruit can give you the tasty shake of your favorite flavor.

ORANGE-STRAWBERRY WAKE-UP (Serves 4)

In a blender container, combine orange juice, strawberries, egg, nonfat milk, and water. Blend until smooth. Pour into 4 glasses and garnish with an orange twist and a fresh strawberry. Serve immediately.

–Mrs. David Sandifer (Jackie)

1 c. orange juice
1 (10 oz.) pkg. frozen strawberries, partially thawed
1 egg
½ c. nonfat dry milk
½ c. cold water

HOT SPICED PERCOLATOR PUNCH (Serves 8-10)

Put pineapple juice and water in bottom part of an 8-cup percolator and the rest of the ingredients in the percolator basket. Perk for 10 minutes or until spices permeate. Serve hot in mugs or punch cups.

–Mrs. Harold Bryson (Judy)

3 c. pineapple juice
3 c. water
½ c. brown sugar, lightly packed
1 t. whole cloves
1½ t. whole allspice
3 sticks cinnamon, broken
¼ t. salt

HOT SPICED TEA (Serves 8)

Bring water to boil. Add tea bags and cinnamon sticks and steep 10 minutes. Remove bags and cinnamon sticks. Add orange juice, lemonade, and sugar. Mix well. Serve hot. Keeps in refrigerator. Just reheat leftovers.

–Dr. Lorene Archer

4 qt. water
4 small tea bags
2 cinnamon stocks
1 small can frozen orange juice
1 small can frozen lemonade
1-1½ c. sugar, to taste

WASSAIL CIDER (Serves 32)

Combine ingredients, heat to boiling. Simmer 5-10 minutes. Remove spiced and serve hot.

–The Committee

1 (6 oz.) can frozen lemonade
4 sticks whole cinnamon
4 qt. apple cider
1 T. whole cloves
½ t. ground allspice

CHARLESTON PUNCH (Serves 20)

Chill: black coffee liquid. Pour coffee over ice cream in the punch bowl. Blend. Add sugar and vanilla and nutmeg to whipping cream and beat. Add to ice cream and coffee in the punch bowl. Blend well. Equally delicious served hot or cold.

–Nelle Davidson

6 qt. coffee (tres noir)
1 qt. coffee ice cream
⅔ c. sugar
2¼ T. vanilla
1 qt. heavy whipping cream
¼ t. nutmeg
1 qt. vanilla ice cream

MOCHA (Serves 150)

Make coffee one day ahead of time. Then before serving, work in ice cream and last, pour in half and half.

–Mrs. Landrum Leavell (Jo Ann)

4 gal. double-strength coffee
1 qt. half and half
3 gal. chocolate ice cream

COFFEE PUNCH (Serves 15-20)

Set aside coffee and chill. Add milk, sugar, salt, and vanilla. Refrigerate. Let ice cream get soft. Pour over coffee and use immediately. *–Mrs. Tom Monroe*

2 qt. coffee
2 pt. milk
1 c. sugar
1 t. salt
1 T. vanilla
½ gal. ice cream

Appetizers and Party Foods

Many of the recipes in this chapter have a double character. They can serve as either appetizers or desserts for a main course or, in combination, make up a satisfying buffet of varied flavors. Since the foods are small in size and can be easily multiplied, they serve well as party foods. See Appendix I, "How to Plan a Party" and "Special Touches," to help create the perfect setting for your party foods.

Choosing an appetizer: When an appetizer is used as a first course, the following are helpful guidelines to consider: for a dinner that includes poultry, ham, or veal, a fruit cocktail is excellent; for a mild dinner, use a spicier appetizer; for a light entree, choose a more filling appetizer. *Serving of appetizers*: As a rule-of-thumb in planning large quantities of canapés or hors d'oeuvres, allow 10 bites per person. Total the number of canapés, hors d'oeuvres, or sandwiches each recipe makes and divide by 10. This will tell you how many guests you can serve.

Hors d'oeuvres are cold or hot appetizers that, unlike canapés, do not have bread or crackers as a base.

For canapés, use firm-textured or one-day-old bread. If neither is available, partially freeze bread before cutting.

It is better to serve a few canapés at one time and to refill as needed, than to serve an enormous array that will eventually become soggy and unappetizing.

Broiled appetizers should be served immediately after they are cooked—piping hot. Those that do not require broiling may be kept hot on hot trays. *Special touches*: Make your appetizers look pretty, but at the same time make them accessible. Appeal to a number of tastes by offering an equal proportion of sweet, nonsweet, and spicy foods.

For an open house, don't put all the food in one room. Decorate

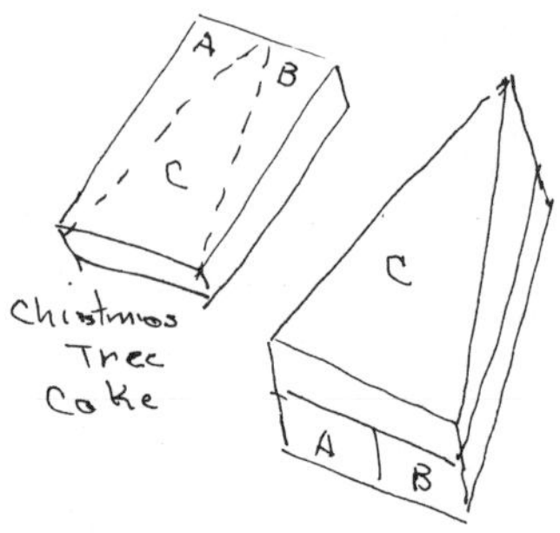

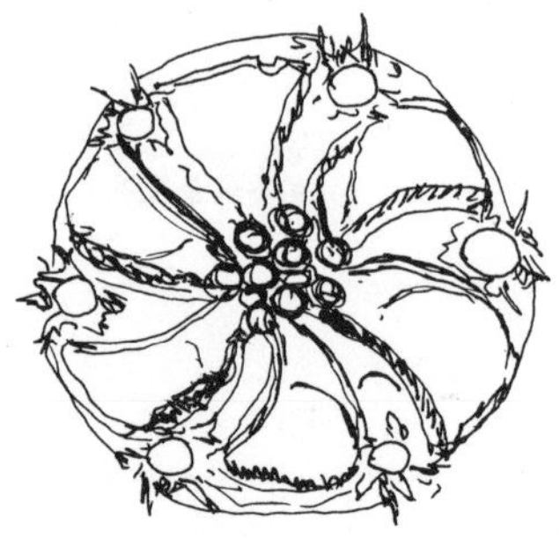

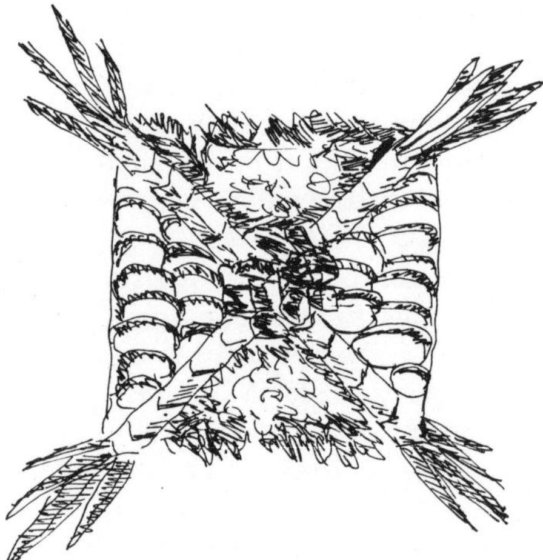

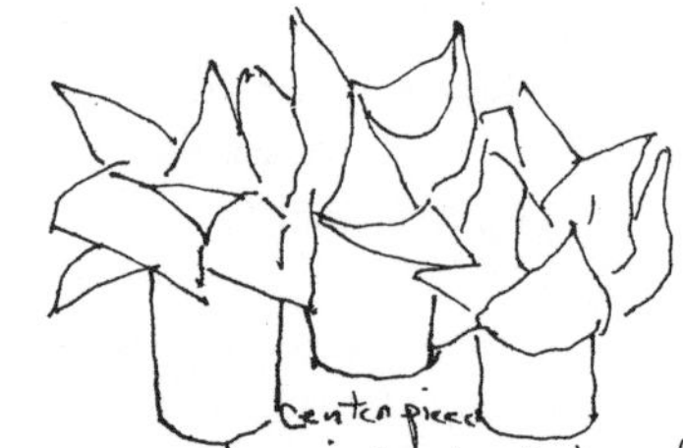

Fill containers with variety of colored napkins

several rooms, and if it is a nighttime gathering, use lots of candlelight. Have one or two finger foods in each room.

To serve crisp vegetables, put ice cubes or crushed ice in a wooden salad bowl or a silver bowl. Put a bowl of dip in the center and arrange raw vegetables on ice. Let guests help themselves.

Eye-catching vegetables such as acorn squash, pumpkins, cabbage, lettuce, and green peppers may be leveled on the bottom, scooped out, and used as containers for dips and appetizers. Pineapple halves, watermelon, and boiled, bleached oyster shells also make good containers.

Here is how to use a cabbage as a serving piece. Square the bottom so that it will sit securely in a shallow bowl or tray. Cut a round hole in the head, large enough to hold a container of shrimp cocktail sauce. Skewer boiled shrimp on picks all around the cabbage.

Pretzels can be used to skewer cheese cubes instead of toothpicks—nothing to dispose of later.

Make diagonal sandwich logs. Remove the crusts from bread slices. Roll the slices flat with a rolling pin. Spread with filling. Then roll bread as for a jellyroll and cut diagonally into two or three parts.

Delectable edible "trees" can be fashioned with the aid of a tall styrofoam cone covered with parsley and studded with shrimp or celery, radishes, carrots, cucumbers, cherry tomatoes, or cauliflower. Secure tidbits to cone with toothpicks and arrange in a spiral motif.

Topiary tree: A topiary effect can be achieved with a styrofoam ball studded with ripe or green olives that have been pitted or stuffed. Arrange almonds or nuts around the base of the tree to simulate pebbles.

Vegetable tree: Use a clay flowerpot and a stick, such as a broomstick, cut to about 12 inches in length. Cover stick with green floral tape. Fill flowerpot with plaster of paris and insert stick. (For a table arrangement, make more than one tree and vary the heights of each by varying the lengths of the broomstick "trucks.") When dry, put a round styrofoam ball on the top. Cover ball with ivy, using straight pins. Then put cherry tomatoes on toothpicks and push into ball. Cover the flowerpot with red foil paper. Add ivy leaves at the base of the stub to hide the plaster of paris. Provide a dip for cherry tomatoes.

JEZEBEL DIP

Mix well in blender and refrigerator overnight. Mixture will appear liquid when blended, but will have a preservelike consistency after being in the refrigerator overnight. Keeps for a long period of time. Have cream cheese at room temperature. Pour Jezebel dip over cream cheese and serve with Ritz or similar cracker. *Variation*: use dip for boiled shrimp, egg rolls, or sausage biscuits. *–Mrs. Ethel D. Caraway*

18 oz. pineapple preserves
¾ small can dry mustard
1 cracked pepper to taste
18 oz. apple jelly
¾ small jar horseradish
1 large pkg. cream cheese

HOT SEAFOOD DISH OR DIP (Serves about 200)

Mix all ingredients in order given and heat simultaneously. Do not let boil. Serve in

3 cans small shrimp
3 cans cream of shrimp soup
3 (15½ oz.) cans king crab

chafing dish with bite-sized pastry cups or melba rounds. *–The Committee*

1 (12 oz.) can tuna
3 T. grated onion
salt and pepper to taste
3 (8 oz.) cartons sour cream
pastry cups or melba rounds

MOCK OYSTER DIP (Serves 25)

Cook broccoli in water until well done. Sauté onion in oleo. Add cream of mushroom soup, mushrooms, and juice. Break up garlic cheese and hot sauce and add to mixture. Add hot sauce and broccoli. Mix well. Keep warm in chafing dish; eat with potato chips or other chips. Can also be used in tiny patty shells for party, or with noodles as a casserole.

–Mrs. Richard C. McLemore (Mary Elizabeth)

1 pkg. frozen chopped broccoli
1 large onion, minced
8 T. butter or margarine
1 can cream of mushroom soup
1 can mushroom stems and pieces
1 (6 oz.) roll of garlic cheese
dash of hot sauce

ZEE'S MEXICAN DIP (Serves 8)

Melt margarine; add flour; cook one minute.

Then add:

NOTE: Dry mustard can be left out without causing radical change in taste.

1 stick margarine
4 T. flour
1 T. paprika
1 T. chili powder
⅛ t. garlic powder
2 T. Jalapeño pepper sauce
½ t. dry mustard
¾ T. cumin
2 c. milk
1 pod pepper
1 lb. blue (American Velveeta) cheese

TUNA PARTY DIP

Combine the ingredients and put in refrigerator to chill. Serve with crackers or potato chips. *–The Committee*

1 (6½-7 oz.) can tuna in oil
½ pkg. (1½ oz.) dehydrated onion soup mix
1 c. sour cream
½ t. Tabasco sauce

CELERY STUFFING

Mix and stuff celery or use as dip.

–Mrs. Harold L. Rutledge (Helen)

1 small pkg. cream cheese
½ c. chopped stuffed olives
2 T. mayonnaise

CURRY DIP

Mix all these together. Use as a dip with crackers, chips, cauliflower, and so on.
–Mrs. Paul Bragg (Ruby)

3 T. mayonnaise
curry to taste (2-3 t.)
1 carton sour cream

SHRIMP CURRY DIP

Mix well together and serve as dip or salad dressing. Delicious with raw cauliflower, broccoli, etc. Use wooden salad bowl filled with crushed ice. Put curry dip in center of bowl. Lay raw vegetables on ice. Keeps everything crisp and cool. *–The Committee*

1 c. mayonnaise
2 T. Worcestershire
1 T. curry powder
3 T. catsup (or to taste)
2-3 T. pickle relish
1 can (or less) shrimp, mashed
dash onion juice

HOT SHRIMP DIP

Soften cheese and oleo to room temperature and beat. Add shrimp with a wooden spoon. Add red pepper. Add onion, salt, and a dash of black pepper. Heat in double boiler. Serve hot in chafing dish. Serve with bugles or crackers. *–Mrs. W. L. Stagg, Jr. (Lula)*

1 (8 oz.) pkg. cream cheese
1 stick oleo
2 or 3 small cans of shrimp, drained
dash red-hot pepper
3 green onions
dash salt and black pepper

AVOCADO CRAB DIP (Serves 6-8)

Drain and flake crab meat. Mash avocados until smooth. Add all other ingredients and mix well. Serve with carrot and bell pepper sticks or crackers. *–Miss Sandi Swartz*

7½ oz. frozen crab meat
1 large or 2 medium avocados
1 T. lemon juice
1 t. Worcestershire
¼ c. sour cream
1 T. grated onion
1 (8 oz.) pkg. cream cheese, softened
¼ t. Accent
¼ t. salt

DILL DIP

Blend all ingredients together and chill. Great for dipping raw vegetables (cauliflower, radishes, carrots, celery, cucumber, broccoli, green onions, and so on).
–Mrs. Lawrence Goff (Linda)

¾ c. mayonnaise
1 T. dry parsley
1 T. Beau Monde seasoning
¾ c. sour cream
1 T. dry chives
1 T. dill weed

HOT CHEESE DIP

Heat cheese with tomatoes and chiles in double boiler until cheese is melted. Serve in fondue or chafing dish to keep hot.

–Mrs. Leroy Yarbrough (Edwyna)

2 lb. Velveeta cheese
1 can tomatoes and chiles

CALIFORNIA COTTAGE CHEESE DIP

Mix together in medium-sized bowl. Serve with uncooked vegetables such as celery, carrots, cucumber, cauliflower, zucchini, mushrooms, turnips, bell peppers, and so on.

–Mrs. Weldon Fortenberry (Georgie)

1 pt. cottage cheese
2 T. onion (chopped fine)
2 t. dill weed
1 c. mayonnaise
2 T. parsley (chopped fine)
2 t. Beau Monde

SHRIMP DIP

Mix all ingredients. Let sit to combine flavors. Good with crackers! NOTE: Mrs. Leavell hollows out a half a pineapple and serves the dip in the pineapple shell.

–Mrs. Landrum Leavell (Jo Ann)

2 (8 oz.) pkg. cream cheese
juice of 2 lemons
1½ or 2 T. onion juice
Tabasco to taste
1½ lb. cooked shrimp, chopped up
2 T. chile sauce
1 T. Worcestershire sauce
½ c. mayonnaise

ARTICHOKE BALLS (Serves 40)

Fry onion and garlic in olive oil and drain. Mix artichoke hearts and bread crumbs. Add eggs and mix thoroughly. Add onions, garlic, and cheese. Mix thoroughly. Refrigerate one hour. Form balls and roll in mixture of ⅓ cup bread crumbs and ⅔ cup grated Italian cheese. Refrigerate until serving time.

–Mrs. John McPherson (Marie)

½ t. chopped onion
2 T. olive oil
1 (14 oz.) can artichoke hearts, drained and mashed
1 c. seasoned bread crumbs
2 eggs, beaten until fluffy
¼ c. grated Italian cheese
3 cloves garlic, crushed or garlic powder

CHEESE STRAWS I (Yields 12-14 dozen)

Place grated cheese and butter in large mixing bowl. Let sit until soft. Cream with mixer and add garlic. Gradually add flour,

1 lb. grated cheese
1 stick butter
1 clove garlic, pressed
½ t. salt

salt, and red pepper. Mix well. Blend in sesame seeds. Use cookie press to make straws. Bake at 350° for 13 minutes.

–Mrs. Claude L. Howe (Joyce)

¼ t. red pepper
1 box sesame seed

CHEESE STRAWS II

Cream butter and cheese together. Add flour, salts, Tabasco. Squeeze through cookie press or roll into logs and slice ¼-½ inch thick. Bake in a slow oven, 300 °, until crisp.

–Mrs. Larry Barlow (Lynne)

1 stick butter
1 lb. sharp cheddar cheese, grated
2 c. flour, sifted
½ t. garlic salt
Tabasco, to taste
½ t. salt

SAUSAGE AND CHEESE BALLS

Mix ingredients together and form into small balls. Bake at 350 ° until brown (about 10 minutes). If desired, part of dough can be put into freezer and cooked later.

–Mrs. Jason Archer (Carolyn Lee),
Mrs. Skip Archer (Catherine),
Mrs. John McPherson (Marie)

1 lb. sausage
1 lb. sharp cheese, grated
3½ c. biscuit mix

CHEESE BALLS

Mix above ingredients. Form into a ball. Save half of pecans to go outside.

–Mrs. Landrum P. Leavell (Jo Ann)

2 (8 oz.) pkg. cream cheese
1 (1 oz.) blue cheese
1 T. chopped pimento
1 c. chopped pecans
1 (8 oz.) pkg. mild cheddar cheese
1 T. grated onion
1 T. green pepper
½ c. chopped parsley (on outside)

CHEESE CRACKS

Mix above in order given. Form into small balls and press with fork. Bake at 350 ° or until light brown.

–Mrs. Tim Williams (Glennis)

2 sticks oleo
2 c. grated sharp cheddar
½ t. salt
2 c. plain flour
2 c. Rice Krispies
½ t. red pepper

MINIATURE CREAM PUFFS (Makes 4-6 dozen)

Pour water into a saucepan; add butter, and bring to a boil. Reduce heat; add flour all at once, stirring rapidly. Cook and stir until mixture thickens and leaves sides of pan, about 2 minutes. Remove from heat. Add eggs, one at a time, beating thoroughly after each addition. Then beat until mixture looks satiny and breaks off when spoon is raised. Drop by teaspoonfuls, about 1 inch apart, onto an ungreased baking sheet. Bake at 425° for 30 minutes or until done. Cool.

1 c. boiling water
1 c. all-purpose flour
½ c. butter
4 eggs

Deviled Cheese Filling (yields about 1 cup):

Mix all ingredients together; split cream puffs and fill.

1 c. shredded American cheese
3 T. mayonnaise
1 t. grated onion
¼ t. dry mustard
½ t. Worcestershire sauce
5-6 drops Tabasco sauce
½ t. celery seed

Shrimp-Cheese Filling (yields about 1 cup):

Mix all ingredients together; split cream puffs and fill. Garnish with paprika if desired.

½ c. (5 oz.) flaked cooked shrimp
1 T. freshly squeezed lemon juice
¼ c. shredded sharp Cheddar cheese
1 T. chopped pimento
3 T. mayonnaise
salt and pepper to taste
paprika (optional)

Blue Cheese Filling (yields about 1 cup):

Cream blue-cheese spread (softened) until smooth. Blend in Worcestershire sauce. Fold in sour cream; chill. Split cream puffs and fill. Top with a little of the filling or a sprinkling of paprika or minced parsley, if desired. *–The Committee*

1 (5 oz.) jar blue cheese spread, soft
½ c. commercial sour cream
1 t. Worcestershire sauce
paprika (optional)
minced parsley (optional)

CHEESE NIBLETS

Cream butter. Add other ingredients. Shape in rolls. Refrigerate until firm. Cut in about

½ c. oleo
2 c. grated sharp cheese
¾ c. finely chopped nuts

¼-inch thickness. Bake at 350° for 10 minutes. You may decorate with pecans or paprika. *–Mrs. W. L. Stagg, Jr. (Lula)*

¼ tsp. cayenne pepper
1 t. salt
1 c. flour

SHRIMP SANDWICH SPREAD

Mix above in order and spread on open-faced bread rounds.
–Mrs. Landrum Leavell (Jo Ann)

1 lb. ground shrimp
2 T. mayonnaise to soften cream cheese
3 oz. cream cheese
grated onion
ground pickles

PARTY BREAD FILLINGS

Combine all ingredients; mix well. Set aside and later spread on bread slice.

½ c. cooked, diced chicken
1 T. minced onion
½ t. salt
⅛ t. pepper
½ c. chopped celery
2-3 T. mayonnaise
½ t. curry powder
1 (4 oz.) can sliced mushrooms, drained

Deviled Salad (1 cup):

Combine all ingredients; mix well. Set aside and later spread on bread slice.

1 (3 oz.) can deviled ham
1 T. pickle relish
2-3 T. mayonnaise
2 hard-cooked eggs, chopped

Creamy Nut (1 cup):

Combine all ingredients; mix well. Set aside and later spread on bread slice.

1 (3 oz.) pkg. cream cheese
1 c. chopped nuts
4-6 T. light cream
Pinch of salt

Frosting:

Combine cream cheese and cream. Reserve nuts for garnish after sandwich loaf is frosted.

3 (3 oz.) pkg. cream cheese
½ c. light cream
1 c. chopped nuts

Mushroom-Chive-Cheese (1 cup):

Combine mushrooms and cream cheese until smooth.

¼ c. canned mushrooms, chopped
⅓ c. chive-flavored cream cheese

Creamy Orange-Pecan (1¼ cups):

Combine all ingredients and mix well.

2 (3 oz.) pkg. cream cheese
4 T. orange juice
2 T. grated orange rind
1 c. chopped pecans

Apricot-Almond (1½ cups):

Combine all ingredients and mix well.

1 c. stewed dried apricots.
½ c. chopped almonds
1 T. grated orange rind

Spicy Ham 'n Raisin (1½ cups):

Combine all ingredients and mix well.

1 (4½ oz.) can deviled ham
¼ c. chopped nuts
½ c. chopped celery
2 T. mayonnaise
¼ c. chopped raisins

Walnut-Smoked Cheese (⅔ cup):

Combine all ingredients and mix well.

–The Committee

¼ c. chopped walnuts
½ t. Worcestershire sauce
¼ c. smoked cheese spread
¼ c. mayonnaise

PARSLEY WHEEL SANDWICHES

Combine cream cheese with cream. Add other ingredients and mix well. Using small cookie cutter, cut circles from thin-sliced fresh bread. Spread with cream cheese mixture. Roll edges of sandwiches in finely chopped parsley. Garnish each sandwich with dot of egg yolk, finely mashed.

–Mrs. Fred Mosley (Gay)

1 (3 oz.) pkg. cream cheese
1 T. cream
1 t. onion, grated
½ t. Worcestershire sauce
dash of Tabasco
1 t. lemon juice
food coloring, if desired

COCKTAIL WIENERS (Serves 12)

Mix prepared mustard and currant jelly in chafing dish or saucepan over low heat. Slice 1 pound (8-10) frankfurters diagonally in bite-sized pieces. Add to sauce and heat thoroughly. TIP: Make ahead. It improves the flavor. It can be frozen.

–Mrs. Harold Bryson (Judy)

1 (6 oz.) jar prepared mustard
1 (10 oz.) jar currant jelly
1 lb. frankfurters or smoked sausage

BARBECUED MEATBALLS

Combine all ingredients and make small balls. Brown in grease, drain, and simmer in oven at 450° for 40-45 minutes.

1 lb. ground beef
½ c. fine bread crumbs
½ c. applesauce
1 egg

Sauce:

Combine ingredients in order and simmer. Add meatballs. Heat.

–Mrs. Gary Hadden (Marilyn)

1 c. catsup
1 T. vinegar
1 T. sugar
1 c. water (or as needed)
2 T. chopped onion
1 T. Worcestershire sauce
2 T. Heinz 57 sauce

SWEET-SOUR MEATBALLS

Mix together, roll into balls. Cook at 350° for 1½-2 hours.

1-2 lb. ground beef
1 finely chopped onion
½ c. barbecue sauce
1 t. salt
1 t. pepper
1 t. garlic salt
¼ c. sugar

Sauce:

Bring all ingredients to boil. Add 1 tablespoon cornstarch in cold water to thicken and then pour over meatballs. Serve over yellow rice or with toothpicks as appetizers.

–Mrs. Genter Stephens (Dot)

1 c. sugar
½ c. vinegar
1 T. chopped pimento
1 green Tabasco pepper
½ c. water

PARTY MEATBALLS (Makes 225 meatballs)

Mix ingredients well and roll into bite-sized balls. Fry in about ½ inch of oil. Drain and place in baking dish about 2 inches deep.

4 lb. ground chuck
1 lb. sausage (hot, if desired)
4 slices stale bread, soaked in milk
2 white eggs, beaten
1 medium-sized white onion (grated or put through blender)
garlic salt
salt and pepper
parsley flakes

Sauce:

Mix all ingredients and simmer in skillet for 25 minutes. Pour sauce over meatballs. Simmer in oven at 350° for about 30 minutes. Freezes well. *–The Committee*

1 medium onion (grated or finely chopped)
4 T. brown sugar
2 c. water
1 T. prepared mustard
½ c. lemon juice
4 T. oil
2 c. catsup
4 T. vinegar
salt

MEATBALLS

Thoroughly mix all ingredients except the barbecue sauce. Shape mixture into ½-inch balls; place in large skillet and bake for 30 minutes in 350° oven. Pour off liquid and gently stir meatballs. Bake another 30 minutes, stirring occasionally or until lightly browned. Remove from oven and pour barbecue sauce over meatballs. Cool, stir once or twice. Put in covered container in refrigerator overnight. Heat before serving. Serve from chafing dish.

–Mrs. John F. Gibson

1 lb. lean hot sausage
1 c. finely chopped onion
1 t. salt
1 T. soy sauce
2 lb. lean ground beef
1 finely chopped garlic clove
1 t. crushed red pepper
1 c. barbecue sauce

HEAVENLY HASH POPCORN (Makes 2½ quarts)

Spread popcorn on buttered jellyroll pan or baking sheet. Sprinkle with the marshmallows and peanuts. Arrange chocolate bars on top. Put in preheated oven for 5 minutes. Cool slightly. Toss in a bowl or container.

–Mrs. James Bradfield (Paula)

Preheat oven to 300°
2 qt. unsalted popped popcorn
½ c. salted peanuts
1 c. miniature marshmallows
9 (¾ oz.) bars milk chocolate

APRICOT-COCONUT BALLS

In a large mixing bowl blend together apricots and coconut. Stir in condensed milk. Shape into small balls and roll in sugar. Let stand at room temperature until firm. These may be kept in a covered container in refrigerator for days.

–Mrs. W. L. Stagg, Jr. (Lula)

1½ c. (6 oz.) ground dried apricots
2 c. moist coconut
confectioners' sugar, if desired
⅔ c. (7½ oz.) Eagle Brand sweetened condensed milk

CRESCENTS (Makes 5 dozen)

Mix all ingredients. Let sit in refrigerator for a few hours or until firm. Roll in hands to make small crescent-shaped pieces. Bake at 300° until light brown. Makes about 5 dozen. *–Mrs. W. L. Stagg, Jr. (Lula)*

2 heaping T. powdered sugar (may need to add more)
1 c. nuts, chopped fine
1 c. flour
1 T. water
½ t. vanilla

DATE-CREAM CHEESE ROLL-UPS (Makes 8 dozen)

Cream butter and cheese together. Blend in flour and salt. Chill for several hours or until firm enough to roll. Roll to ⅛-inch thickness on board sprinkled with confectioner's sugar. Cut in 1-by-3-inch strips with pastry wheel. Put a date in center of each strip and roll up. (You can put a pecan piece in each date). Put folded side down on cookie sheets. Bake in moderate oven (375°) for about 15 minutes. If desired, sprinkle with confectioner's sugar. Makes about 8 dozen. This same recipe can be used for tart shells.

–Mrs. W. L. Stagg, Jr. (Lula)

1 c. butter (oleo)
½ lb. cream cheese
2 c. sifted flour
¼ t. salt
confectioner's sugar
pitted dates

FILLING FOR TART SHELLS (SWEET) (Makes 2 dozen)

Melt the above ingredients in a double boiler. When melted, add ½ cup coconut. Pour in tart shells. Serve with whipped cream or Cool Whip. Variations: pecan pie filling, chicken salad filling, or tuna salad.

–Mrs. W. L. Stagg, Jr. (Lula)

4 Mars bars
2 T. butter
2 T. milk

COCONUT LOAF CAKE

Cream butter and Crisco. Add sugar and cream well. Add eggs one at a time, beating well. Mix flour, baking powder, and salt. Add alternately with milk. Add flavoring and coconut. Put in greased and floured tube or long loaf pan. Bake at 300° for 1 hour. Cool before moving from pan. NOTE: Serve on a long silver tray if cooked in long loaf pan.

–Mrs. W. L. Stagg, Jr. (Lula)

2 sticks butter
½ c. shortening
3 c. sugar
5 large or 6 small eggs
2 t. coconut flavoring
1 c. sweet milk
3 c. flour
½ t. salt
½ t. baking powder
2 cups fresh or packaged coconut

CHOCOLATE SURPRISE (Serves 15-18)

1 cup flour
1 stick oleo, melted
½ cup nuts, chopped fine

1 (8 oz.) pkg. cream cheese
1 c. Cool Whip
1 c. powdered sugar

Pour oleo over flour and nuts. Spread over bottom of a 9-by-13-inch pan. Press into all corners. Be sure the entire bottom of the pan is covered. Bake at 375° for 15 minutes. Cool 1 hour. Set aside.

Mix and pour over pie crust. Then mix 2 small packages instant fudge pudding with 3 cups cold milk. Pour over cream cheese mixture. Chill. Before serving, spread remainder of Cool Whip on top. Sprinkle on ground pecans for garnish. Serves 15-18.

–Mrs. W. L. Stagg, Jr. (Lula)

PECAN TASSIES (Makes 2 dozen)

1 pkg. cream cheese (3 oz.)
½ c. butter or margarine
1 c. sifted all-purpose flour

Let cream cheese and ½ c. butter or margarine soften at room temperature; blend together. Stir in flour. Chill about one hour. Shape in 2 dozen 1-inch balls; place in ungreased 1¾-inch muffin pans. Press dough against bottoms and sides.

Pecan Filling:

1 egg
1 T. soft butter or margarine
1 drop almond extract
¾ c. brown sugar
1 t. vanilla
dash of salt
⅔ c. coarsely broken pecans

Beat together egg, brown sugar, and the 1 tablespoon butter or margarine, the vanilla, almond extract, and salt just until smooth. Divide half the pecans among pastry-lined pans, add egg mixture, and top with remaining pecans. Bake in slow oven (325°) for 25 minutes or until filling is set. NOTE: Pastry can be used with other fillings.

–Mrs. Carroll B. Freeman (Hellon)

PARTY STRAWBERRIES (Makes about 100)

5 T. butter (not margarine)
2½ c. rice krispies (do not crush)
1 c. sugar
red sugar crystals
stems*
1½ c. chopped dates

Use an electric skillet. Melt butter on warm heat. Stir in eggs combined with sugar. Add dates. Increase temperature to 360°. Cook for 5 minutes, stirring constantly. Turn off heat. Add salt and vanilla. Stir well. Add

rice krispies and nuts. Working quickly, shape into strawberries. (The mixture will be hot so butter your hands for easier shaping.) As each berry is shaped, roll in red sugar crystals and insert green stem. It is better to have a helper for the shaping and rolling procedures.
*Strawberry stems may be ordered from: Maid of Scandinavia Co., 3255 Raleigh Avenue, Minneapolis, Minnesota 55416, Toll free No. 1-800-328-6722
—Mrs. Harold Bryson (Judy)

1 t. vanilla
dash salt
2 beaten eggs
1 c. chopped nuts

LEMON SQUARES

Mix ingredients in order given. Bake in 8-inch pan for 15 minutes at 350°. Remove from oven and spread with: 1 cup sugar, ½ teaspoon baking powder, ½ teaspoon salt, 2 eggs and 2 tablespoons lemon juice and rind. Bake at 350° for 20 minutes. Cool and ice with 3 tablespoons lemon juice, ¾ cup powdered sugar, and 1 tablespoon melted butter.
–Mrs. Chuck Kelly (Rhonda)

¼ c. confectioner's sugar
⅛ t. salt
1 c. plain flour
½ c. melted butter

PECAN MERINGUES (Yields 3 dozen)

Line cookie sheet with plain white paper; beat egg whites, salt, and cream of tartar until frothy. Add sugar gradually, beating until stiff peaks form. Fold in pecans and vanilla. Drop by teaspoonfuls onto lined cookie sheet. Bake at 300° for 25 minutes.
–Mrs. Fred Mosley (Gay)

2 egg whites
⅛ t. salt
⅛ t. cream of tartar
¾ c. sugar
⅔ c. finely chopped pecans
1 t. vanilla

ORANGE BALLS (Yields 6 dozen)

Crush vanilla wafers into fine crumbs. Add sugar, margarine, orange juice, and nuts and mix well with hands. Form into balls.

1 (12 oz.) pkg. vanilla wafers
1 stick margarine softened
1 c. finely chopped nuts
1 (1 lb.) box powdered sugar

Chill until firm and store in refrigerator. Roll balls in coconut immediately after shaping. These may be frozen for up to six months if desired.

–Mrs. Tom Monroe (Simone)

1 (6 oz.) can thawed orange juice concentrate
1 pkg. flaked coconut

SAND TARTS

Cream butter and sugar. Add flour, nuts, vanilla. Bake on greased cookie sheet in 300° oven until brown. Sprinkle with sugar.

–Mrs. Landrum Leavell (Jo Ann)

½ lb. butter
2 T. confectioner's sugar
add vanilla
2 c. flour added to butter and sugar
2 c. nuts

Roland Q. Leavell Chapel

Joy Rust

Soups and Sauces

Oversalted soup may be desalted by slicing a raw potato into it. Boil for a short time, then remove potato.

Add a slice of lemon or a piece of orange peel when making soups. It will give the soup an unusual and delightful flavor.

To make pure *celery salt*, put leaves from celery stalk into a pie plate and place in warming oven to dry. When dry, roll on a piece of paper until very fine. Put into a salt shaker and use instead of celery salt. It is excellent for soups.

Dress up your favorite soup with *colorful garnishes* such as these: popcorn, toasted croutons, crisp cereal, minced parsley, lemon slices, hard-cooked egg slices, chopped nuts, and shredded cheese.

Do you ever run out of *catsup*? If so, combine 1 cup tomato sauce or mashed canned tomatoes, ¼ cup packed brown sugar, 2 tablespoons vinegar, ¼ teaspoon cinnamon, and a dash each ground cloves and allspice.

Soup as a sauce: In our busy lives, condensed soups find their way to our table in the form of tasty sauces. These can be used in a variety of ways, such as sauces to serve over meat, fish, vegetables, rice, toasted sandwiches, and with crackers. They are equally useful as base for casseroles. Heat the undiluted soup slowly and thin with a little milk or consommé if it is too thick, then season to taste. Basic soups such as celery, mushroom, onion, tomato, and cheese can be experimented with as sauces.

Sauces should blend or contrast in flavor with the vegetable with which they are to be served. They should be smooth and not too thick.

If you need just one or two tablespoons *Hollandaise* for a sauce or glaze, you can use a good quality mayonnaise (not creamy dressing).

Sauces are best when served immediately. If for any reason they are not, be sure to beat them well with a hand beater, such as a wire whisk. Be sure to use a wooden spoon for delicate sauces that may be broken down by the more vigorous metal tools.

If your *gravy is too thin*, mix some water and flour, cornstarch or arrowroot to a smooth paste. Stir into the gravy and bring to a boil, stirring constantly. If a gravy thickened with cornstarch or arrowroot becomes too thin, it's probably been overcooked. Re-thicken with more cornstarch or arrowroot; cook just until thickened again. Remove from heat.

If your *gravy is too pale,* color with a few drops gravy seasonings, browning sauce, or soy sauce. To avoid the problem in the first place, brown the flour well before adding liquid. This will also help prevent lumpy gravy.

Freeze *leftover vegetables* in plastic containers in your freezer. Dump vegetables and their juices in these containers until several are full. Buy ham chunks or freeze a little leftover ham and combine all of this with canned tomatoes, cubed potatoes, frozen sliced okra. Simmer several hours for the yummiest soup ever.

BASIC WHITE SAUCE

Thin:
2 T. butter
1 T. flour
¼ t. salt
1 c. milk

Medium:
3 T. butter
2 T. flour
½ t. salt
1 c. milk

Thick:
4 T. butter
3-4 T. flour
½ t. salt
1 c. milk

Melt butter in small saucepan and stir in flour and salt. Blend until smooth and add milk. Turn to low heat, stirring constantly. Cook just below boiling point to desired consistency (thin sauce: cream soups; medium sauce: vegetables, chicken, or fish; thick sauce: croquettes or souffles). *VARIATIONS*: *Cheese sauce*: Add 1 cup grated American cheese to 1 cup hot medium sauce. Season with dash cayenne pepper or Worcestershire sauce or both. *Horseradish sauce*: Add ¼ cup prepared horseradish, 2 teaspoons lemon juice, and ¼ teaspoon paprika to 1 cup hot medium white sauce. *Mushroom sauce*: Add ½ cup chopped, cooked mushrooms and ½ teaspoon Worcestershire sauce to 1 cup hot medium white sauce.

–The Committee

BASIC ROUX

In heavy iron skillet blend flour into drippings; place over low to medium heat, stirring constantly until dark brown. Turn off heat; continue stirring. Add boiling water, stirring constantly until smooth and the desired consistency. This roux may be refrigerated for later use. *–The Committee*

⅔ c. flour
¾ c. bacon drippings or salad oil
boiling water

BASIC BROWN GRAVY

Melt butter, remove from heat, and blend in flour. Stir and cook over moderate to low heat until roux has browned. Remove from heat and add basic brown stock. Cook slowly until sauce has thickened. Makes 1¾ cups. *–The Committee*

½ stick butter
4 T. flour
2 c. brown stock
salt and pepper to taste

CHILI (Serves 6)

Brown meat. Add onion, celery, and bell pepper. Add other ingredients and stir. Cook one hour, adding water if necessary. Turn heat off and add lemon juice, stirring well. *–Mrs. Hugh Tobias (Marie)*

2 lb. ground beef
2 cans red beans
2 bottles chili sauce
1 small can chili powder
¼ c. chopped onion
¼ c. chopped celery
¼ c. chopped bell pepper
4 T. lemon juice (add last)
salt and pepper

SHRIMP CREOLE I (Serves 6)

Cook onion, green pepper, and celery in the salad oil until tender but not brown. Add tomatoes, tomato sauce, Worcestershire sauce, salt, sugar, chili powder, and hot pepper sauce. Simmer uncovered 45 minutes. Boil shrimp and drain. Mix 2 teaspoons cornstarch with 1 tablespoon cold water; stir into sauce and cook until bubbly. Add shrimp and green pepper. Cover and cook on low about 15 minutes. Cook about 2 cups of

½ c. chopped onion
½ c. chopped celery
½ c. chopped green pepper
3 T. salad oil
16 oz. can tomatoes
8 oz. can tomato sauce
1 T. Worcestershire
1½ t. salt
1 t. sugar
1 t. chili powder
½ t. hot pepper sauce
16 oz. fresh or frozen shrimp

rice separately and drain. After shrimp and sauce are done, mix the rice and sauce together. With a tossed salad and French bread, this makes a great meal.

–Mrs. Melvin J. Poole (Linda)

SHRIMP CREOLE II (Serves 6-8)

3 stalks celery, chopped
½ green pepper, chopped
1 small onion, chopped
1 clove garlic, minced
4 T. shortening
1 T. Worcestershire sauce
1 t. Tabasco sauce
1 lb. shrimp, shelled and deveined
1 t. lemon juice
1 (28 oz.) can tomatoes
1 (10½ oz.) can tomato soup

Cook celery, green pepper, onion, and garlic in shortening until tender. Add remaining ingredients, except shrimp. Simmer for 30 minutes. Add shrimp and simmer for additional 30 minutes. Serve over rice.

–Margaret Stewart

SHRIMP GUMBO (Makes 8 quarts)

(A) Chicken (3 pounds)

1 t. poultry seasoning
1 t. marjoram
1 t. sage
1 t. thyme
2 t. salt

Cover chicken with water in large pot. Add seasonings. Boil gently until tender. Remove from broth and let cool. Reserve broth. Remove chicken from bones and cut in bite-sized pieces. Refrigerate.

(B) Shrimp (½ gallon)

Peel shrimp and rinse in cool water. Drain and refrigerate.

(C) Vegetables

1 large bell pepper, chopped
2 large onions, chopped
1 lb. chopped okra (fresh or frozen)
4 stalks celery, chopped
3 cloves garlic, chopped

(D) Roux

Combine ½ cup oil and ¾ cup flour. Stir continually. Cook in large skillet until *very dark brown.* Add okra and cook, stirring about 2 or 3 minutes. Add other vegetables (group C). Stir about 5 minutes. Have chicken broth hot. Add roux and vegetables. Stir.

(E) Add: 4 bay leaves, 1 teaspoon black pepper, ¼ cup parsley flakes, 1 can tomato sauce, 12 ounces tomato paste, 1 pound can mashed-up tomatoes. Stir. Cook over low heat. Add shrimp and chicken. Add salt to taste. Simmer 3-4 hours. Stir occasionally. Let cook. Package and freeze. (Better if prepared one week before serving.) Serve over rice. *–Mrs. Ray Robbins (Louise)*

SEAFOOD GUMBO (Serves 6-8)

2 lb. cooked shrimp
2 T. oil
2 T. flour
3 c. okra, chopped or 1 T. filé
2 chopped onions
2 T. oil
1 can tomatoes
2 qt. water
1 bay leaf
1 t. salt
red pepper (optional)

Peel uncooked shrimp and devein. Make dark roux of flour and oil. Add shrimp to this for a few minutes, stirring constantly. Set aside. Smother okra and onions in oil. Add tomatoes when okra is nearly cooked. Then add water, bay leaf, salt, and pepper. Add shrimp and roux to this. Cover and cook slowly for at least 1 hour. If okra is not used, add gumbo filé after turning off heat. Serve with rice. Gumbo is seasoned better if cooked the day before serving. If done this way, save filé for when it is reheated.

–Mrs. Fisher Humphreys (Caroline)

CREOLE CHICKEN GUMBO (Serves 10)

1 hen or large stewing chicken
½ c. shortening or cooking oil
2 lb. okra, fresh or frozen
1 medium-sized onion
1 large clove garlic
1 green pepper
2 qt. chicken stock
1 bay leaf
1 rib celery, chopped
1 T. finely chopped parsley
1 T. Worcestershire sauce

Boil chicken in salted water until tender. Save chicken stock and add enough water to make 2 quarts. Chop chicken into small pieces and return to the pot with the stock. Put shortening in a saucepan and heat. Add onions and garlic and sauté until golden brown. Add green pepper and okra. Fry until all the "ropiness" is gone. Add this to pot with chicken. Pour tomato sauce into the saucepan and stir and scrape pan, removing all the browned particles. Add this to pot along with seasonings and celery. Simmer slowly for 2 hours. Add parsley about 15 minutes before serving. Serve hot over fluffy rice.

salt and pepper to taste
1 can tomato paste

–Mrs. Tom DeLaughter (Lurlean)

MY MOTHER'S CHICKEN SOUP (Serves 4-6)

Cover small chicken (cut in pieces) or left-over chicken parts with water. Add salt. Simmer until meat falls easily from the bone. Remove chicken and add about 4 carrots and 4 stalks of celery cut in thin pieces. Cook slowly until tender. Add meat from chicken and enough noodles to make as thick as you like it. (Add more water while vegetables are cooking, if needed.) Cook slowly until noodles are done. Salt and pepper to taste. A package of chicken gravy mix can be added if you don't have much chicken. Rice may be used instead of noodles.

–Mrs. Early Taylor (Judy)

POTATO SOUP

1 pkg. frozen hashbrowns
salt and pepper to taste
1 onion, cut fine
¾ stick butter

Barely cover hashbrowns with water. Cook until tender (until onion is done.) Set off and let cool before you pour milk in. Pour in milk (about 1-1½ cups). Heat and serve.

–Mrs. Paul Earley (Jackie)

UNIQUE CHICKEN SOUP (Serves 6)

1 fryer
2 large cans tomatoes
2 pkg. frozen creamed corn

Cover fryer with water and season with salt to taste. Cook. Remove fryer; skin and debone. Add tomatoes, corn, and chicken to stock in which the chicken was cooked. Simmer about 2 hours. Immediately before serving add a little milk (about 2 tablespoons per bowl). It adds just a special touch.

–The Committee

QUICK VEGETABLE SOUP (Serves 6)

Brown beef and onion in margarine. Drain. Add remaining ingredients and cook on low for 2 hours. Serve with crackers or corn bread.

–Mrs. Perry Neal

1 lb. ground beef
1 large onion
½ stick oleo
1 large can tomatoes
1 tomato can of water
2 boxes frozen lima beams
salt and pepper to taste

BARBECUE SAUCE I

Melt butter in pan over low heat. Sauté onions until tender, add catsup, brown sugar firmly packed, Worcestershire sauce, and salt; stir in chili powder, pepper, and Tabasco. Simmer about 15 minutes or less. Any leftover sauce may be refrigerated several days.

–Mrs. Mike O'Brien (Nita)

½ c. butter
½ c. catsup
3 T. Worcestershire sauce
1 t. chili powder
½ c. chopped onion
¼ c. light brown sugar
1 t. salt
⅛ t. pepper
dash of Tabasco

BARBECUE SAUCE II

Combine ingredients and simmer 10 minutes.

–Mrs. Tim Williams (Glennis)

1 c. vinegar
2 T. Worcestershire sauce
½ c. catsup
1 clove garlic
½ t. Tabasco sauce
1 t. salt
1 T. dry mustard

BARBECUE SAUCE III

Bring all ingredients to a boil. Pour in jar. Store in refrigerator. Keeps indefinitely. Store in a 20-ounce catsup bottle.

–Mrs. "Skip" Archer (Catherine)

20 oz. catsup
1 generous T. Worcestershire sauce
1 T. Tabasco sauce
3 T. prepared mustard
1 t. season salt
⅓ c. water
1½ T. liquid smoke
1 t. vinegar
1 t. garlic salt
2 t. chili powder
1 cup firmly packed brown sugar

TOP OF STOVE BAR-B-Q

Pour over meat and bring to a quick boil; cut heat to low. Cook one hour or until meat is tender.

–Mrs. Aaron Ray (Linda)

1 c. barbecue sauce
1 c. coke
2 lb. chicken or pork chops

KUMBACK SAUCE (Makes 2 pints)

Mix together and refrigerate. Delicious on cold fish or green salads.

–Mrs. John McPherson (Marie)

2 garlic cloves, grated (or garlic powder)
1 onion, grated
1 c. mayonnaise
¼ c. catsup
¼ c. chili sauce
1 t. mustard
½ c. oil
1 T. Worcestershire
1 t. black pepper
2 T. water, if needed
dash horseradish

SHRIMP SAUCE

Mix well in jar and chill. Serve in small bowls.

–Mrs. Ray Robbins (Louise)

1 c. catsup
½ c. salad dressing
1 t. prepared mustard
2 shakes hot sauce

SWEET AND SOUR SAUCE

Heat mixture to a boil. Add bell pepper. Thicken with cornstarch paste. Use as a glaze for Polynesian or barbecue sauce over shrimp, pork, or chicken.

–Mrs. Fred Mosley (Gay)

½ c. catsup
½ c. vinegar
½ c. sugar
2 T. soy sauce
1 small can pineapple chunks
1 T. cornstarch in 3 T. water
½ c. pineapple juice
½ bell pepper, diced

CUCUMBER RELISH

Cover with vinegar. Add sugar last. Put in glass fruit jars. Seal tightly and place in refrigerator. Will keep up to 3 months.

–Mrs. George Tumlin (Lynda)

2 qt. grated cucumbers (squeeze out juice, then measure)
8 finely chopped onions
1 lb. (2 c.) sugar
2 T. black pepper
1 t. red pepper
3 T. salt

Salads

When *selecting lettuce,* do look for a head that is heavy for its size; don't buy lettuce with brown spots.

To store *clean salad greens,* wrap in a damp cloth, waxed paper, or special storage bag; or place the greens in the covered hydrator of your refrigerator.

If salad greens are wet when they are combined with dressing, the *moisture on the greens* will prevent the leaves from becoming coated with dressing.

To prevent *wilting and soggy salads,* dry greens before combining with dressing.

Add *variety to salads* with shredded cabbage, Chinese cabbage, spinach, young leaves from mustard greens or other tender greens, nasturtium leaves, and the leaves from wild plants such as dandelions.

Some salad materials offer more *nutritive values* than others. For example, salad plants with green leaves and stalks contain about ten times more vitamin A than those with bleached or pale leaves and stalks; carrots that have a bright, deep yellow color furnish more vitamin A than pale yellow ones.

Use your freezer to give *an extra chill to sliced fruits.* Place them in the freezer 15 minutes or so before serving. Don't expose salad greens to freezing temperatures; they will wilt.

When there is not enough liquid in a recipe *to both soften and dissolve gelatin,* soften the gelatin in cold water in the top of a double boiler; then place over boiling water and stir until the gelatin is thoroughly dissolved.

To unmold gelatin dishes, dip mold in warm water to the depth of the gelatin, loosen around the edges with the tip of a paring knife, place serving dish on top of mold, and turn upside down. Shake, holding serving dish tightly to the mold. If gelatin does not unmold readily, repeat.

Sellars Building

Cafeteria

To center a gelatin mold on a serving plate, smooth a few drops of water on a plate with fingers; unmold gelatin as usual. The film of water will allow just enough slippage to move the mold. (Dip mold in lukewarm water for only a few seconds (10 or so) to remove the gelatin easily.)

APPLE SALAD (Serves 12)

Grate 6 apples. Sugar to sweeten. Drain in colander. When ready to serve on lettuce leaf, fold in two sliced bananas. Garnish with sweetened whipped cream and sprinkle chopped nuts and place a cherry on top. This is the traditional Thanksgiving dinner salad at the Dodd home.

–From the files of the late Mrs. M. E. Dodd, submitted by her granddaughter Mrs. Joyner (Virginia)

Virginia writes: "My grandfather, the late Dr. M. E. Dodd, had a hand in the organizing of the Seminary and I would like to submit two of my grandmother's recipes. The Administration building of the old campus was named after my grandfather, and on the present campus, a dormitory is named after him."

BLUEBERRY SALAD (Serves 12-14)

2 (3 oz.) pkg. blackberry jello
1 small can crushed pineapple
½ c. sugar
1 can blueberries
1 (8 oz.) pkg. cream cheese
½ c. chopped nuts

Dissolve jello in water as directed on package. Add blueberries and pineapple, including juices. When congealed, add topping.

Topping:

Soften cream cheese; add sugar and sour cream and blend until smooth. Spread on salad and sprinkle with chopped nuts.

–Mrs. Robin W. Arflin

FRUIT SALAD

Mix all together and chill.

–Faculty Workshop, 1976

2 pkg. prepared whipped topping
1 c. coconut
1 c. chopped nuts
1 small can fruit cocktail, drained

FROZEN BANANA SALAD

Mix all together and freeze.

–Mrs. Bill Hinson (Bettye)

1 large can crushed pineapple
1 pt. sour cream
1 c. chopped nuts
1 c. sugar
½ c. chopped maraschino cherries
3 large mashed bananas or 2 T. lemon juice

FROZEN WALDORF SALAD (Serves 12)

Combine eggs, sugar, pineapple juice, lemon juice, and salt and cook over low heat until thick, stirring constantly. Cool. Add celery, pineapple, apples, and nuts. Gently fold in whipped cream. Spoon into 8-inch square pan or line muffin pan with paper cups and freeze.

–Mrs. Chester Vaughn (Evelyn)

2 eggs, slightly beaten
½ c. sugar
½ c. pineapple juice
¼ c. lemon juice
⅛ t. salt
½ c. celery, chopped fine
½ c. crushed pineapple, drained
2 medium-sized apples, chopped
½ c. chopped nuts
1 c. whipped cream or 1 small container prepared whipped topping

CHERRY SUPREME SALAD

After mixture has cooled, fold in: 1 cup whipped cream, 1 cup tiny marshmallows, and ½ cup chopped nuts.

After first mixture has congealed, add second mixture to it. Congeal. Cut in squares and serve on lettuce.

–Mrs. Paul Stevens (Glenda)

Mixture one:
Mix and congeal:
1 pkg. cherry jello
1 c. boiling water
1 can cherry pie filling

Mixture two:
Mix and cool:
1 pkg. lemon jello
1 c. boiling water
1 can crushed pineapple
1 (3 oz.) pkg. softened cream cheese
⅓ c. mayonnaise

COCO-COLA SALAD

Drain juice from cherries and pineapple into saucepan; bring to a boil and mix with both packages of jello. Dissolve jello 5-10 minutes. Dump jello and cream cheese into mixer. Put into big bowl and add Coca-Cola. Mix pineapple, cherries, and nuts with mixture and pour into mold. Refrigerate 4-6 hours. *–Mrs. Bill Hanks (Jandy)*

1 small pkg. wild strawberry jello
1 (16 oz.) bottle of Coca-Cola
1 (20 oz.) can crushed pineapple
1 small pkg. black cherry jello
3 small pkg. cream cheese (softened)
1 large can black cherries (or fresh)
½ lb. pecans (more or less)

FROSTED FRUIT SALAD

Dissolve lemon and orange jello in hot water. Add cold water and lemon juice. Chill slightly. Add drained pineapple, bananas, and marshmallow bits. Chill.

1 pkg. lemon jello
1 pkg. orange jello
2½ c. hot water
½ c. cold water
juice of one lemon
1 large can crushed pineapple, drained
2 bananas, diced
1 c. marshmallow bits

Topping:

Mix and cook until thick, flour, sugar, egg, pineapple juice, and butter. Cool. Mix whipped topping according to package directions. Add these two mixes together and spread on top. *–Mrs. Howard Alford (Kay)*

1 egg, beaten
1 c. pineapple juice
2 T. butter
1 small pkg. Dream Whip

FROZEN CHRISTMAS SALAD

In a mixing bowl, blend together sour cream, dessert topping, sugar, lemon juice, and vanilla. Fold in fruit and nuts. Turn into 4½-cup ring mold. Freeze several hours or overnight. Unmold onto lettuce and garnish with additional cherries. Let stand 10 minutes before serving. *–Mrs. Bill Hanks (Jandy)*

1 c. sour cream
½ (2¼ oz.) small carton Cool Whip
½ c. sugar
2 T. lemon juice
1 t. vanilla
2 medium bananas, diced
1 (13 oz.) can crushed pineapple,drained
½ c. red candied cherries, sliced
½ c. green candied cherries, sliced
½ c. nuts, chopped pecans or walnuts
lettuce leaves

LUSCIOUS JELLO SALAD (Serves 12-15)

1 (15 oz.) can blueberries
1 (8½ oz.) can crushed pineapple
2 c. boiling water
1 large pkg. black cherry jello

Drain blueberries and pineapple and save juice. Add the boiling water plus 1 cup of juice from fruit. After this has cooled slightly, add fruit and let it congeal in an 8-by-12-inch pyrex dish.

Topping:

1 (8 oz.) pkg. cream cheese
½ c. sugar
½ pt. sour cream
1 t. vanilla

Soften cream cheese to room temperature. Beat all ingredients until well mixed. Spread on jello salad. Refrigerate. Either pecans or cherries (maraschino) may be added to jello.

–The Committee

ORANGE MOUNTAIN (Serves 6-8)

1 (9 oz.) carton Cool Whip
1 (3 oz.) pkg. orange jello
1 (16 oz.) cottage cheese
1 (13 oz.) can crushed pineapple
1 can mandarin oranges
2-3 mashed bananas
2-3 c. miniature marshmallows
½ c. chopped pecans

Mix Cool Whip and dry jello until jello is dissolved; add cottage cheese; mix. Add well-drained fruit, mix. Add marshmallows and pecans. Chill.

–Mrs. Paul Hugger (Vickie)

PINEAPPLE BISQUE (Serves 16)

1 small box lemon jello
1¼ c. hot juice and water
⅓ c. sugar
½ t. salt
3 T. lemon juice and rind
1 medium can crushed pineapple
1 large can chilled condensed milk
½ c. vanilla wafers, crushed

Mix jello, water, and juice. Add sugar, salt, and 1 tablespoon lemon juice. Let chill. Then whip and add pineapple. Whip milk with rest of lemon juice and rind in a large bowl. Add jello mixture and beat together. Line 9-by-13-inch glass casserole with crushed vanilla wafers. Pour in jello mixture and spread on remaining crumbs. Chill at least four hours before serving. Best to chill overnight.

–Mrs. Carol Daniels

PEACH-PINEAPPLE CHEESE DELIGHT SALAD

Dissolve jello in hot water and fruit juice. Let mixture cool and gel a little. Add fruit. Place marshmallows on top. Use oblong pyrex dish.

2 pkg. orange jello
2 c. hot water
1 large can peaches, drained and chopped
1 large can crushed pineapple, drained
1 can peach and pineapple juice, combined
¾ c. miniature marshmallows

Topping:

Combine sugar and flour. Beat in egg; stir in juices. Cook over low heat, stirring until thick. Remove from heat, stir in butter or margarine. Cool. Fold in cream and spread over firm jello mixture. Sprinkle with cheese. *–Mrs. Edwin Quattlebaum (Betty)*

¼ c. sugar
3 T. flour
1 egg, slightly beaten
1 c. combined juices
2 T. butter or margarine
1 c. heavy whipping cream (or Dream Whip or Cool Whip)
¾ c. grated cheese

FRESH CANTALOUPE FRUIT SALAD (Serves 6)

Combine cantaloupe, pineapple, strawberries, and dressing to taste. Toss lightly. Serve on chilled lettuce.

–Mrs. Paul Stevens (Glenda)

2 c. diced cantaloupe
1 c. fresh pineapple wedges
1 c. sliced fresh strawberries
French salad dressing

GREEN COTTAGE CHEESE SALAD

Dissolve both packages jello in 2 cups boiling water. Cool. Cream cottage cheese with mayonnaise. Add milk and pineapple. Stir in jello and add nuts. Refrigerate. NOTE: This will keep in the refrigerator 2 weeks and can also be frozen. It can be altered such as more or less cottage cheese, or leave out nuts, add chopped celery, etc.

–Mrs. Franklin Atkinson

1 (3 oz.) pkg. lime jello
2 (3 oz.) lemon jello
1 (16 oz.) pkg. cottage cheese
1 c. mayonnaise
1 can condensed milk
1 (20 oz.) can crushed pineapple
1 c. nuts

DESSERT OR SALAD

Mix all together and chill thoroughly before using. It can be frozen and used as dessert or salad.

–Mrs. Roland Q. Leavell (Lilian)

1 can strawberry, blueberry, or cherry pie filling
1 small can crushed pineapple
1 large carton Cool Whip
½ c. chopped pecans
1 can Bordens sweetened condensed milk

PINK ARCTIC SALAD (Serves 10)

Mix well. Use an 11¾-by-7½-by- 1¾-inch dish. Freeze 8 hours.
–Mrs. Richard McLemore (Mary Elizabeth)

2 (3 oz.) pkg. cream cheese
4 T. sugar
1 (1 lb.) can whole cranberry sauce
1 c. whipped cream
2 T. mayonnaise
½ c. chopped pecans
1 (9 oz.) can crushed pineapple, undrained

FROZEN SALAD (Serves 20-24)

Blend above ingredients in blender. Fold in 1 large size Cool Whip. Freeze in any container—paper muffin cups are nice for small servings. Insert popsicle stick for children. *–Mrs. Landrum P. Leavell (Jo Ann)*

5 bananas
1 c. sour cream
1½ c. sugar
1 small can crushed pineapple
½ c. lemon juice
chopped pecans
1 pkg. small frozen strawberries

FROZEN CRANBERRY SALAD OR MISSISSIPPI FROZEN SALAD (Serves 18-20)

Whip cream cheese. Add mayonnaise, sugar, and pineapple. Add cranberries and nuts. Fold in whipped cream. Pour in mold and freeze. (This is an excellent salad for individual servings. It may be poured into a muffin pan, then frozen and emptied into a plastic bag for freezer storage.) Serve on lettuce leaves. *–Mrs. Bob Golden (Mary)*

2 (3 oz.) pkg. cream cheese
½ c. chopped pecans
½ pt. whipped cream
1 can whole cranberries (whole berry cranberry sauce may be substituted)
2 t. margarine
2 t. sugar
1 small can crushed pineapple, partially drained

FROZEN STRAWBERRY SALAD (Serves 10)

Drain and slice strawberries, soften cream cheese. Melt marshmallows in strawberry juice in double boiler. Cool. Add strawberries and pineapple. Cream the cheese until smooth and add mayonnaise. Whip cream and fold into other ingredients. Add vanilla and pour into a loaf pan and freeze until firm. Serve on lettuce.
–Pastor's Conference, 1976

16 large marshmallows
1 c. strawberries
1 (3 oz.) pkg. cream cheese
1 c. whipped cream
2 T. strawberry juice
½-1 c. crushed pineapple
½ c. mayonnaise
½ t. vanilla

CHRISTMAS SALAD (Serves 10-12)

Soften cream cheese at room temperature. Mix cream cheese and pineapple juice until creamy. Add small amount of pineapple, grapes (cut in half), pecans, marshmallows, and whipped cream. Mix. Add remaining portions of ingredients and mix. Top with whipped cream. *–Mrs. Dan Storey (Dale)*

1 large bag miniature marshmallows
1 (8 oz.) pkg. cream cheese
1 large can crushed pineapple
1 c. red grapes
½ c. diced pecans
1 can whipped cream

COTTAGE CHEESE SALAD (Serves 8-10)

(Other fruits may be substituted for the mandarin oranges; other flavors may be substituted for the jello.) Cook mandarin oranges over medium heat about 5 minutes, stirring constantly. Sprinkle the jello powder into the hot oranges and mix well. Let cool. Add cottage cheese; fold in Cool Whip. Pour into dish or mold. Refrigerate overnight. VARIATIONS: strawberries and strawberry jello, peaches and peach jello, blackberries and blackberry jello.

–Margaret Stewart

1 small can mandarin oranges
1 (3 oz.) pkg. orange jello
1 (12 oz.) carton lowfat cottage cheese
1 small carton Cool Whip

GINGER ALE SALAD (Serves 10-12)

Bring juices from orange, lemon, pineapple, and cherries to a boil. Dissolve jellos in this mixture. Add grated rind. Add chilled ginger ale. Allow to set in refrigerator until thick. Add cherries, pineapple, and nuts.

1 (3 oz.) pkg. orange jello
1 (3 oz.) pkg. lemon jello
grated rind of one lemon
grated rind of one orange
1 small can crushed pineapple
1 jar Royal Anne cherries (cut in half, seeds removed
juice of one lemon
juice of one orange
½ c. chopped pecans
2 c. chilled ginger ale

Topping:

Mix sour cream with a small amount of mayonnaise. Add a little sugar and grated orange rind. Drizzle over top of each piece just before serving.

–Mrs. Tim Williams (Glennis)

MARSHMALLOW-ORANGE SALAD (Serves 6)

Dissolve jello in 1 cup of boiling water. Add sour cream and pineapple, stir until smooth. Add marshmallows and place in refrigerator until congealed.

–Mrs. Thomas H. Moody (Melba)

1 small box orange jello
½ pt. sour cream
1 small can crushed pineapple
1 c. miniature marshmallows

FROSTED JELLO SALAD

Dissolve the jello in the 2 cups boiling water. Then add the ½ cup cold water, lemon juice, and drained can of pineapple. Add remaining ingredients.

2 (3 oz.) pkg. black cherry jello
2 c. boiling water
½ c. cold water
juice of 1 lemon
1 can crushed pineapple, drained
1 c. miniature marshmallows
1 c. pecans
2 large bananas, diced

Topping:

Mix the pineapple juice, flour, butter, and sugar; cook until moderately thick. Let it get cold. Then prepare Dream Whip as directed on package, mix with cooked mixture, and spread on top of jello salad.

–Mrs. Wayne Hoggle (Romie)

juice of pineapple, 1 c.
2 T. flour
2 T. butter
½ c. sugar
1 pkg. Dream Whip

GRAPE SALAD

Combine: 1 package grape jello and 1 cup hot water.

Add: 1 (6 ounce) can frozen grape juice, 1 cup crushed pineapple, drained well, 1 cup chopped celery, and ½ cup chopped nuts.

Topping: One package Dream Whip and cream cheese, whipped together.

–Mrs. Carol Daniels

FIVE-CUP SALAD, OR MILLIONAIRE SALAD

Mix everything together and refrigerate for several hours or overnight.

–Mrs. Francis Sylvest, Sr.

1 small can mandarin oranges, drained well
1 small can crushed pineapple, drained well
1 small can coconut
1 c. miniature marshmallows
1 c. commercial sour cream

LEMON CONGEALED SALAD

Dissolve jello in 2½ cups of boiling water and set aside to cool. Combine cream cheese, mayonnaise, pineapple and juice, nuts, marshmallows, and vinegar. Add to jello and pour in shallow pan to congeal.

–Nita O'Brien

3 small pkg. lemon jello
1 (15½ oz.) can crushed pineapple in own juice
1½ c. chopped nuts
2 (8 oz.) pkg. cream cheese
1 c. mayonnaise
2 c. miniature marshmallows
½ t. vinegar

WATERGATE SALAD (Serves 8)

Mix dry pudding mix and *undrained* pineapple. Add remaining ingredients, mix well, and chill.

–Mrs. Billy E. Simmons (Flo)

1 box pistachio pudding and pie filling mix
1 (20 oz.) can crushed pineapple
½ c. chopped nuts
1 (9 oz.) carton Cool Whip
1½ c. small marshmallows

LURLINE'S FRUIT SALAD

Mix all together and chill overnight.

–Mrs. John McPherson (Marie)

1 can cherry pie filling
1 can condensed milk
large can crushed pineapple
7 oz. coconut
1 (9 oz.) carton Cool Whip
2 c. chopped nuts

HOT CURRIED FRUIT (Serves 6-8)

Drain juice from all fruit the day before. Mix fruit, juice, sugar, curry powder and arrange in 1½-quart casserole. Bake (covered) at 325° for one hour. At the end of baking, add orange and lemon rind. Bake another 10 minutes (uncovered).

–Mrs. Richard C. McLemore (Mary Elizabeth)

1 (39 oz.) can peach halves
1 (39 oz.) can Bing cherries
½ c. brown sugar
¼ c. orange juice
1 (39 oz.) can apricot halves
1 medium can pineapple chunks
1 t. curry powder
rind or ½ orange and ½ lemon

BAKED APRICOTS (Serves 8)

In greased baking dish layer above ingredients, ending with crackers. Bake in slow oven at 300° for 45 minutes. NOTE: Baked apricots can be a vegetable dish also.

–Mrs. Russell McIntire (Maellen)
Mrs. James Richardson

1 large can apricots
6 oz. Ritz crackers
1 box light brown sugar
1 stick butter

SCALLOPED PINEAPPLE (Serves 8)

Drain pineapple and place juice in boiler; over low heat add flour and sugar, stirring constantly until thick. Place pineapple and grated cheese in buttered casserole. Pour cooked mixture over this and blend well. Dot with butter; bake at 325° for 30 minutes.

–Mrs. Joe H. Tuten

1 (20 oz.) can crushed pineapple
½ c. flour
butter
½ c. sugar
½ lb. mild Cheddar cheese

CONGEALED CARROT SALAD (Serves 10-12)

Empty crushed pineapple and sugar into pot and bring to a boil. Dissolve gelatin in cold water, pour into pineapple, and set aside to cool. Grate carrots and add to cooled gelatin; add cottage cheese and whipping cream (do not whip too hard). Pour into mold or 11-by-15-inch dish.

–Mrs. Clyde Price (Lynda)

1 medium-sized can crushed pineapple
1 c. sugar
2 envelopes unflavored gelatin
½ c. cold water
1 c. grated carrots
1 (12 oz.) carton small curd cottage cheese
½ pt. whipping cream

GUACAMOLÉ SALAD

Place layer of chopped lettuce and 1 slice of tomato on each salad plate. Top with about 2 tablespoons guacamolé dip. (This may be a prepared frozen dip or a homemade mixture of 2 avocados with ¼ cup Picante sauce, 1 tablespoon lemon juice, and salt to taste made in blender.)

–Mrs. Leroy Yarbrough (Edwyna)

CORN RELISH SALAD (Serves 4-6)

In a large bowl combine macaroni, corn, celery, green pepper, onion, and tomatoes. Combine sauce, garlic, and oil and oregano; blend and pour over salad. Add salt. Toss to blend and chill for several hours.

–Donna Garner

2 c. cooked macaroni, cooled
2 (12 oz.) cans kernel corn, drained
2 c. sliced celery
1 green pepper, chopped
1 medium onion, chopped
2 medium tomatoes, chopped
1 clove garlic, mashed
¼ c. salad oil
½ t. oregano
1 (7 oz.) can green chile sauce or taco sauce
salt to taste

PIQUANT LIMA BEAN SALAD (Serves 6-8)

Cook lima beans according to package directions, drain. Combine remaining ingredients; toss with lima beans. Refrigerate at least 8 hours before serving.

–Mrs. Bradford Curry (Catherine)

2 (10 oz.) pkg. frozen lima beans
1 dill pickle, diced
½ c. commercial sour cream
2 T. lemon juice
1 c. diced celery
4 green onions, chopped
¼ c. mayonnaise
2 T. prepared horseradish
pimento to garnish

MARINATED VEGETABLE SALAD

Drain the mushrooms, artichoke hearts, and baby carrots. Combine all seasonings in small saucepan and bring to a boil. Cool slightly. Pour over vegetables. Cover and refrigerate 12 hours or longer.

–Mrs. John McPherson (Marie)

2 cans sliced mushrooms
1 can artichoke hearts, cut up
1 can baby carrots
2 T. pimento, chopped
⅔ c. white vinegar
⅔ c. olive oil
1 t. sugar
½ c. minced onion
1 T. Italian seasoning
1 t. salt
¼ t. minced garlic
⅛ t. black pepper

SLAW

Bring first six ingredients to a boil, then cool. Then pour over the remaining vegetables. Mix well; place in the refrigerator for 12 hours before serving. Will keep well for a week or more.

–Mrs. James B. Brown (Edna)

1 pt. vinegar
1 t. mustard seed
1 t. tumeric
2½ c. sugar
1½ t. celery seed
1 t. salt
1 large cabbage (shredded)
1 green pepper, diced
2 medium onions, chopped
1 small can pimento or 2 red peppers

SAUERKRAUT SALAD (Serves 12-14)

Heat water, vinegar, and oil; dissolve sugar in hot liquid. Pour dressing over vegetables and mix well. Chill. This salad is very crisp and has a grand flavor. Best of all, it keeps indefinitely.

–Mrs. Fisher Humphreys (Caroline)

Combine:
2 (16 oz.) cans sauerkraut
1 c. diced celery
1 c. diced green peppers
1 large jar pimento, chopped
1 c. chopped onion
1 small can water chestnuts, sliced

Mix:
⅔ c. vinegar
⅓ c. water
⅓ c. oil
1¼ c. sugar

TOMATO ASPIC (Serves 10)

Dissolve lemon jello in tomato juice, heated to the boiling point. Add cold tomato juice, salt, celery, pepper, pecans, and minced onions to taste. Pour into mold and congeal.

–Mrs. Harold Bryson (Judy)

1 small pkg. lemon jello
¾ c. cold tomato juice
½ c. chopped celery
1 c. heated tomato juice
¼ t. salt
⅓ c. chopped bell pepper
½ c. pecans and minced onions

GREEN LAYER SALAD (Serves 15-20)

Sprinkle 2 packages Italian cheese dressing mix over top, and seal with mayonnaise. Refrigerate 12-24 hours. Mix and toss with one diced avocado just before serving. (NOTE: Use only Hellman's mayonnaise.)

–Mrs. James Richardson

Toss Together:
1½-2 heads lettuce
1 cauliflower, broken in flowerets (or 1 pkg. frozen cauliflower)
1 small bunch green onions (tops included)
1 pkg. frozen English peas, cooked and drained
Hellman's mayonnaise

FRESH SPINACH SALAD

Tear spinach leaves in bite-sized pieces. Add other ingredients except for dressing and toss together. Just before serving, heat dressing and pour over salad.

–Mrs. John Watson (Jory)

fresh spinach
8 slices bacon, crumbled
zesty Italian dressing
1 can mandarin oranges, drained
croutons

MIXED PEA SALAD (Serves 6)

Mix mayonnaise or salad dressing and French dressing. Add drained peas and chill 2 hours, until flavors blend. Mix with celery and cheese. Season to taste. Serve on lettuce.

–Mrs. Paul Stevens (Glenda)

½ c. mayonnaise or salad dressing
1 c. canned peas
¼ c. French dressing
1 c. sliced celery or carrots
½ c. diced American cheese

24-HOUR SALAD (Serves 15-20)

In a large bowl that can be sealed, layer all ingredients in the order listed. Seal bowl. Refrigerate 24 hours. Toss just before serv-

1 head lettuce, torn in small pieces
½ c. chopped green pepper
½ c. chopped celery

ing. Recipe can easily be adjusted to serve fewer people.

–Mrs. "Skip" Archer (Catherine)

½ c. chopped onion (optional)
1 pkg. frozen green peas, uncooked
¾ c. mayonnaise mixed with ¼ c. sour cream
6 oz. shredded sharp Cheddar cheese
bacon bits

OVERNIGHT VEGETABLE SALAD (Serves 10)

Pour dressing over vegetable mixture. Chill 24 hours.

–Mrs. Billy E. Simmons (Flo)

Vegetable mixture:
Mix:
1 (20 oz.) can English peas, drained
1 (20 oz.) can French style beans, drained
1 (20 oz.) can whole kernel corn, drained
1 c. celery, diced
½ c. green pepper, diced
1 medium purple onion, diced
1 (2 oz.) jar pimentos, cut
salt to taste

Dressing:
Combine:
1½ c. white sugar
1 c. vinegar
2 t. water
¼ t. paprika
½ c. salad oil

TUNA CURRY SALAD (Serves 6)

In medium mixing bowl, combine all ingredients; mix well. Chill before serving. Serve on lettuce. If desired, garnish with additional chopped walnuts.

–Mrs. Hardee Kennedy (Virginia)

2 (6 oz.) cans tuna, drained and flaked
1 medium stalk celery, chopped
¼-½ t. curry powder
½ c. mayonnaise
¼ c. walnuts, chopped
1 T. onion, chopped
¼ t. salt
1 t. lemon juice
1 (13½ oz.) can pineapple tidbits, drained

MEXICAN SALAD (Serves 12-14)

Shred the lettuce, grate the cheese, and have the beans chilled and drained. Dice tomatoes; chop onions fine. Add the dressing and chilled beans to the above ingredients;

1 large head lettuce
2 medium tomatoes
¾ bottle Kraft Catalina dressing
1 lb. Cheddar cheese
½ onion

chill 30 minutes to an hour before serving. Add crushed Fritos immediately before serving.

–Mrs. Landrum P. Leavell (Jo Ann)

1 large pkg. Fritos
1 (15 oz.) can ranch-style beans

THOUSAND ISLAND DRESSING (Makes About 2 cups)

Mix ingredients in the order given and chill thoroughly before serving.

–Mrs. Carroll B. Freeman (Hellon)

1 c. mayonnaise or salad dressing
3 T. chili sauce or catsup
1 T. chopped sweet pickle or relish
2 T. chopped stuffed olives
1 hard-boiled egg, chopped
½ t. grated onion
½ c. French dressing

POPPY SEED DRESSING

In a small bowl combine the honey, salt, vinegar, and mustard. Gradually add the salad oil, beating thoroughly until the mixture is well blended. Stir in the poppy seeds. Put into a pint jar, cover, and chill for several hours before serving. Shake well before mixing into salad.

–Mrs. Tom Monroe (Simone)

⅓ c. honey
2 T. vinegar
¾ c. salad oil
1 t. salt
1 T. prepared mustard
2-3 t. poppy seeds

Cheese and Eggs

The only way to learn about cheese is to eat it and cook with it. The magic of its flavor added to many dishes can transform an ordinary meal into an epicurean delight!

Fruit accompanies cheese with flair. Use seasonal fruits such as pears or apples, especially with Provolone.

In choosing your *fruits for a cheese board,* make your choice from grapes, pears, apples, plums, or any other fresh fruit that can be eaten gracefully with the fingers. All fruits served on the cheese board should be well chilled; do not remove them from the refrigerator until the moment you are ready to serve.

Cheese can be used for *dessert* and adds a gourmet touch to a meal.

Cheese is delicious when *served with unsalted crackers* or a crusty French bread, toasted or untoasted.

Cheese is *a high-protein food.* Most of the calcium and phosphorous of milk are retained in cheese; sulphur and iron are present; and it is an excellent source of vitamin A, thiamin, riboflavin, and pantothenic acid.

To get the *full, rich flavor* of cheese, remove it from the refrigerator several hours before serving.

Cheese should not be kept longer than one month. The firmer the cheese, the longer it will keep in your refrigerator.

Mold will sometimes form on natural cheese. If it is all *surface mold,* wipe with a damp cloth. If the mold is deep, cut it out. This will not affect the taste of the cheese.

You may want to grate your own cheese or buy freshly grated cheese in small quantities. The *best cheeses for grating* are dry and hard—for example, Cheddar, Gruyere, pineapple, and Parmesan.

Italian types of cheese such as Mozzarella and Provolone are good *cheeses for cooking.*

Dodd Building

Joy Rust

One pound of Romano cheese yields approximately 4-5 cups grated cheese.

Cheddar cheese, which is often called American or "store" cheese, is the *standard cooking cheese.* It may be sharp, mellow, or mild in flavor.

Processed cheeses melt nicely to a creamy smoothness in sauces, but they are rather bland in flavor.

Shred cheese on a standard kitchen shredder. Use the medium side.

Always *cook cheese at a low temperature.* Cheese becomes tough or stringy if cooked too fast or too long.

Soufflé: Tie a collar of waxed paper around a soufflé dish. When the soufflé is set and the paper removed, the soufflé will stand high.

Cheese should be stored in a tightly wrapped package in a cool, dry place. Cottage cheese and cream cheese should be stored in the refrigerator and used within a few days.

Cheese making used to be entirely a home industry. In 1851, Jesse Williams began making cheese in a factory in Oneida County, New York. This was the first cheese factory in the United States.

EGGS BENEDICT (Individual servings)

Poach number of eggs desired. Place egg on half of toasted English muffin that has been covered either with crisp bacon or fried Canadian bacon or ham. Cover egg with Hollandaise sauce. Serve immediately!

Quick Hollandaise Sauce (makes ¾ cup):

3 egg yolks
1½ T. lemon juice
A few drops Tabasco

Beat the ingredients in a blender until frothy and thick. In a small saucepan, melt 1 stick of butter to boiling. Pour melted butter in blender slowly. Blend until mixed thoroughly. *–Mrs. Bill Rogers (Louwilda)*

EGG-HAM-POTATO CASSEROLE (Serves 6)

1 small onion, minced
6 T. margarine
6 T. flour
½ t. salt

In saucepan, sauté onion in margarine until golden. Stir in flour, salt, and pepper. Add milk and cook over low heat, stirring until thickened. Add 1 cup cheese and stir until melted. Remove from heat and pour over remaining ingredients, except paprika. Mix gently but thoroughly, then put in shallow 2-quart baking dish and sprinkle with remaining cheese and some paprika. Bake in preheated 400° oven 15-20 minutes or until bubbly. *–Mrs. Ronnie Wright (Sarah)*

¼ t. pepper
1½ c. shredded Cheddar cheese
6 hard-cooked eggs, sliced
2 c. diced, cooked peeled potatoes
1 (12 oz.) can chopped ham, diced
paprika
2½ c. milk

WELSH RAREBIT (Individual servings)

For each serving, put 1 or 2 slices bread or split English muffins in the oven-proof plate; slice cheese to cover bread. Sprinkle with onion slices, add 2 strips bacon and a slice of tomato. Broil until bacon is cooked. Serve with a small pitcher of vinegar to pour over rarebit. NOTE: this is a quickie and is very unusual. Good for Sunday night or when unexpected company comes by.

–The Committee

GORDINE'S PIMENTO CHEESE

Soften cream cheese; add remaining ingredients with enough mayonnaise to make cheese spreadable. *–The Committee*

1 lb. cream cheese
2 lb. hoop cheese, grated
1 large jar pimento, mashed
½ onion, grated
1 rib celery, grated
mayonnaise to taste

SWISS CHEESE PIE

Grate cheese; mix with eggs and cream until smooth and blended. (There will still be some lumps.) Pour into unbaked pie shell and bake in hot oven for 25 minutes. Serve as a main dish for a light meal. Serve with tossed salad and a light fruit dessert.

–Miss Vivian Holder

½ lb. Swiss cheese
2 eggs
½ c. of cream
pastry shell

QUICHE LORRAINE I (Serves 6)

Sprinkle bacon in pie crust. Cover with cheese. Put other ingredients in blender or

9-inch pie shell
4 slices bacon, cooked and crumbled

mixer. Beat well. Pour over cheese. Bake at 350° for 45 minutes. Serve hot. If you don't have enough Swiss cheese, substitute Cheddar or whatever else is available. Use plain milk, if you like, instead of cream. You may add chopped ham or shrimp, crab, or any leftover seafood or meat. *–The Committee*

1½ c. shredded Swiss cheese
4 eggs
1 c. half-and-half
nutmeg
pepper

QUICHE LORRAINE II

Cover pie shell with cheese and ham. Beat eggs and add seasonings. Add milk gradually. Mix well. Pour over ham and cheese. Bake at 375° 50-55 minutes. Let cool 15 minutes on wire rack.

–Mrs. Ray Rust (Joy)

1 pie shell with high fluted edges, uncooked
½ lb. Swiss cheese, grated
1½ c. boiled ham, minced
3 eggs plus 1 yolk
1 t. salt
⅛ t. black pepper
¼ t. nutmeg
3 drops Tabasco sauce
1½ c. milk

MACARONI À LA MUSHROOM (Serves 4)

Fix macaroni and cheese according to box directions. Add the soup to macaroni and mix together. Add milk and stir well. Let warm for about 5 minutes.

–Mrs. George T. Flanagan (Brenda)

1 box macaroni and cheese
1 can cream of mushroom soup
1 c. milk

GARLIC GRITS

Cook grits, boiling water, and salt for 5 minutes. Add to hot grits margarine and garlic cheese (garlic powder if desired). Put eggs in measuring cup and beat well, then finish filling cup with the milk. Add eggs and milk to the grits. Pour mixture into greased casserole. Bake at 350° for 45 minutes. NOTE: Serve at breakfast or as a starch at dinner. Sprinkle with additional cheese if desired.

–The Committee

1 c. quick grits
4½ c. boiling water
1 t. salt
¾ stick margarine
1 tube garlic cheese
garlic powder to taste (optional)
2 eggs
¾ c. milk

CHEESE-BROCCOLI CASSEROLE (Serves 12)

12 slices sandwich bread
12 oz. sharp cheese
2 pkg. frozen broccoli
3 c. diced ham
½ t. dry mustard
½ t. salt
6 eggs, slightly beaten
3 c. milk
2 T. instant onions

Cut bread with doughnut cutter and remove crusts. Place rest of bread in 13-by-9-by-2-inch dish sprayed with vegetable oil. Then put grated cheese, broccoli, and ham into dish. Mix remaining ingredients. Place doughnut bread on top. Bake 55-60 minutes in 325° oven. Let stand 10 minutes before serving. *–Mrs. Ethel D. Caraway*

CHEESE SOUFFLÉ (Serves 6)

8 slices bread, crusts removed
4 eggs
2 c. milk
1 stick butter or margarine
½ lb. sharp cheese, grated

Cut bread into cubes; place in buttered casserole. Beat eggs and add milk. Melt butter; add cheese (melt butter and cheese over hot water). Add to milk mixture. Pour over bread cubes and mix well. Leave overnight in refrigerator (covered). Take out 1 hour before baking. Bake 1 hour at 350°, uncovered. (Any leftover soufflé can be reheated the next day in foil in a slow oven.) NOTE: Serve creamed chicken over soufflé. You can use a soufflé dish or a pyrex casserole.

–Dr. Helen Falls

Meats

POULTRY

If you are feeding a large number of people, turkey meat is the least expensive, and turkey breast yields the greatest amount of protein per pound. Duck yields the least.

Larger birds have more *meat in proportion to bone* and so are often a more economical buy. For each person served, allow ¾-1 pound of chicken, guinea chicken, or turkey; 1-1½ pounds of duck or goose; and 1 pigeon, squab, or small Cornish game hen.

Cut up poultry is more perishable than whole birds; turkey is more perishable than chicken.

If you have bought chicken in *airtight wrappings,* loosen the wrappings before refrigerating.

You may want to salt both the outside and inside of poultry before roasting. Always wait to stuff bird until just before roasting. If a stuffed bird is left out of the refrigerator for too long, the stuffing may spoil.

Marinate poultry or fowl in soy sauce for several hours. Then use your favorite recipe.

Other possible *seasonings for chicken* are thyme, lemon balm, basil, and fresh sage.

Half an hour before roasting time is up, turn back the foil on your bird to let the skin brown prettily.

Before *carving your turkey* or any other bird, let it stand for about 20 minutes.

When *freezing leftover roast poultry,* remove the stuffing and freeze the poultry and stuffing separately. Do not stuff poultry before freezing.

Serve poultry with crisp fried onion rings and rice cooked with toasted, buttered almonds. Cheese grits are delicious served with game.

School of Christian Training

BEEF

Cellophane wrappers on meats sold from self-service meat cases give sufficient protection for *freezer storage* periods of 1-2 weeks only. For longer periods, cover the cellophane with special freezer wrap.

Low *cooking temperature* keeps the juice and flavor of meat intact. It cuts down on shrinkage, keeps the meat more tender and palatable, and prevents burnt fat drippings.

For a roast that is medium rare in the center and well done around the edges, turn the oven to 375° at noon, roast for 1 hour, and turn off the oven. Do not open the door; do not peek. Forty minutes before you are ready to serve, turn the oven back on to 375.

To remove *excess fat* from a skillet of browned meat, tip pan and use a bulb baster or a paper towel folded in several layers to sop up the fat. To remove fat from soup or stew, run an ice cube wrapped in cheesecloth over the surface. If you have the time, of course, the easiest way to remove fat is to refrigerate the soup or stew overnight; the fat will harden and rise to the top; it can then be skimmed off with a spoon.

Onion mums: Here's a way to add a bright note to a meat platter. Peel a medium-sized onion. Cut down from the center into ⅛-inch-wide sections, cutting only about three quarters of the way down the onion. Hold the onion under hot tap water; spread it open gently. Set the onion in water tinted with red or yellow food coloring; use just enough water to cover the onion. Let stand until delicately tinted. Drain.

For main-dish recipes calling for *wine as flavoring*, chicken or beef bouillon may be substituted in the same amount. For desserts in which only a small amount of liqueur or wine is called for, use a big of orange or lemon peel or a drop of vanilla or almond extract. When a larger amount of wine is specified in a recipe, substitute an equal quantity of apple, orange, or grape juice.

To transport a roast or keep it hot for up to one hour, wrap it in a double thickness of foil or in ten or more layers of newspaper.

Refreezing thawed meat? Frozen meat must be kept frozen at 0°F. or less. It is not wise to refreeze thawed meat because of the loss of meat juices during thawing and the possible deterioration of the meat between the time of thawing and refreezing.

WHAT TO SERVE WITH MEATS

Roast pork: Browned potatoes, applesauce, or fruit salad, sweet potatoes, sauerkraut, mashed potatoes, celery or apple salad

Pork chops: Scalloped potatoes, fried apple rings, mashed potatoes, cabbage salad

Baked ham: Sweet potatoes, spinach, rice, pineapple rings, parsley potatoes, asparagus

Cold ham: Baked beans, relish, egg rolls, potato salad, dill pickles

Ham steak: Buttered rice, glazed pineapple, fried eggs, hashed brown potatoes, hominy, corn muffins, fried bananas

Sausage: Fried apples, corn bread, mashed potatoes, pickled peaches

Veal cutlet: Baked potato, tossed salad

Lamb chops: Buttered parsley potatoes, succotash, browned potatoes, spinach, peas

Roast lamb: Mashed potatoes, currant jelly

Liver: Bacon, corn bread

Ground beef: Roasted hamburger buns, sweet onion rings, potato salad, carrots

Meat loaf: Baked potato, canned tomatoes, French fried potatoes, asparagus

Roast chicken: Candied sweet potatoes, cauliflower

Fried chicken: Lima beans, mashed potatoes, corn on the cob, biscuits

Chicken fricassee: Dumplings, corn on the cob

Chicken pie: Green peas, tossed salad

Chicken salad: Potato chips, celery, pickles, peas

Trout: Potatoes diced in cream, asparagus, pickles

Baked snapper: Broccoli with Hollandaise sauce, mashed potatoes, tossed salad

Lobster: Steamed clams, baked potato

French fried shrimp: Mixed vegetables, tomato and onion salad

Broiled fillets: Baked potatoes, scalloped tomatoes

Filet of sole: Cole slaw or dill pickles, tartar sauce

Baked salmon: Baked potato, tossed salad, greens

Fried fish: French fried potatoes, tossed salad

GLAZED FRUITED CHICKEN (Serves 4)

1 (29 oz.) jar fruits for salad
⅔ c. mayonnaise
1 (7 oz.) pkg. herb stuffing
1 fryer, cut up
½ t. salt
1 (12 oz.) jar orange marmalade

Drain fruit; set aside. Reserve ⅔ cup of liquid. Stir reserved liquid into mayonnaise. Stir constantly over medium heat until mixture boils. Add stuffing. Spread in 13-by-9-by-2-inch pan. Add chicken. Sprinkle with salt. Arrange fruit around chicken. Brush on marmalade. Bake 15 minutes.

–Mrs. James Blakney (Jan)

CHICKEN SUPREME (Serves 6)

6-7 whole chicken breasts, halved and deboned
2 c. sour cream
4 t. Worcestershire sauce
2 t. paprika
2 t. salt
¼ c. lemon juice
2 t. celery salt
1 clove garlic, minced
½ t. pepper

Mix all ingredients well except chicken. Wash breast and wipe dry. Dip and coat in mixture. Place in covered pan in refrigerator overnight. Roll in bread crumbs (about 2 cups). Arrange in shallow pan so pieces don't touch. Pour ½ cup melted oleo over top. Sprinkle with paprika. Bake at 350° for one hour.

–Mrs. Paul Robertson (Judy)

CHICKEN WITH CHEESE SAUCE (Serves 3-4)

3-4 chicken breasts
3-4 slices bacon
3 T. butter
3 T. flour
1 t. salt
2 c. milk
¼ c. Parmesan cheese, grated
½ c. Cheddar cheese, grated

Arrange chicken skin side up in large dish; top with one piece bacon and bake at 400° for 25 minutes. Spoon off fat. Meanwhile, melt butter in saucepan and stir in flour and salt until smooth. Gradually stir in milk and cook (while stirring) until mixture thickens. Gradually add both cheeses to the mixture and spoon over chicken. Broil several minutes, or until lightly browned.

–Mrs. Chuck Kelley (Rhonda)

CHICKEN TETRAZZINI (Serves 12-15)

Boil hen and save broth. Bone chicken and skim fat off broth. Use this fat to sauté the bell pepper. Make white sauce using 1 stick butter, 1 quart of milk, and 4 tablespoons cornstarch. Add both kinds of cheese, sautéed bell pepper, mushrooms, pimento, parsley, and chicken to sauce. Salt and pepper to taste. Cook 1 package egg noodles in broth until tender. Drain and layer in baking dish with white sauce. Sprinkle some Parmesan cheese on top and bake in 325° oven for 45 minutes. This dish may be prepared days ahead, frozen, and popped into the oven when ready to eat.

–Mrs. Carl A. Hudson (Dottie)

1 large stewing hen
½ lb. (1 c.) American cheese, grated
1 large can Parmesan cheese
1 bell pepper
1 large can mushrooms
1 can pimento, chopped
1 pkg. egg noodles
parsley

THREE-SOUP CHICKEN (Serves 8)

Melt margarine; add three soups (undiluted); then stir in rice, mushrooms, and water. Pour into 9¼-by-13-inch pan. Salt chicken and place over rice mixture. Bake at 275° for 1½ hours, then turn chicken and continue cooking for 1 hour.

–Mrs. Chester Vaughn (Evelyn)

1½ sticks margarine
1 can cream of mushroom soup
1 can cream of chicken soup
1 can cream of celery soup
1¼ c. rice (uncooked)
1 small can mushroom pieces, drained
½ can water
8 chicken breasts or a fryer cut up

CHICKEN AND RICE (Serves 6-8)

In a pan mix soup, nutmeg, and water. Add raw rice to soup mixture and stir. Lay chicken on top, skin side up. Dribble butter across top. Sprinkle each part of chicken with salt and paprika. Cover with foil and put in 250° oven for 2½ hours. Remove foil and turn to 350° and let cook about ½ hour more. Let sit about 10 minutes before serving.

–Mrs. Bill Hinson

1 c. cream of mushroom soup
1 c. cream of chicken soup
1 c. cream of celery soup
¼ t. nutmeg
¼ c. water
1 c. rice, uncooked
chicken pieces
¼ c. melted margarine
salt and paprika

CHICKEN AND YELLOW RICE

Brown chicken in olive oil. Add chopped onions, bell pepper, and garlic, and fry until brown. Add salt, pepper, bay leaf, and tomato. Cook a few minutes on low heat. Add rice and water and bring to a boil. Dissolve saffron in a little water and add to rice. Place in preheated 400° oven and cook for 30 minutes covered. Garnish with peas and parsley.

–Mrs. Roland Q. Leavell (Lilian)

2½ lb. fryer
½ c. olive oil
2 onions, chopped
1 green pepper
1 clove garlic
2 T. salt
¼ t. pepper
1 bay leaf
1 small can tomatoes
2½ c. rice
5 c. water
½ t. saffron
1 c. peas
parsley, for garnishing

BISCUITS AND CHICKEN (Serves 5)

Preheat oven to 425°. Rinse peas to separate. Heat peas, chicken, soup, sour cream, milk, salt, and pepper to boiling, stirring frequently. Prepare rolled biscuits as directed on package. Pour hot chicken mixture into baking dish, 11¾-by-7½-by-1¾-inches, and sprinkle with cheese. Place biscuits on cheese. Bake until peas are tender, about 20 minutes. *–Mrs. Cecil Brasell (Candy)*

1 (10 oz.) pkg. frozen peas
2 c. cut-up cooked chicken
1 (10¾ oz.) can condensed cream of chicken soup
½ c. sour cream
½ c. milk
½ t. salt
⅛ t. pepper
rolled biscuits from mix
1¼ c. shredded Cheddar cheese

CHICKEN WITH DRIED BEEF (Serves 6)

In the bottom of a shallow casserole, arrange dried beef. Wrap a strip of bacon around each chicken breast; arrange over beef. Spread undiluted soup over chicken, cover with aluminum foil and bake in a 300° oven for 2 hours; increase heat to 350°, uncover and bake another 20-30 minutes, basting several times.

–Mrs. J. Hardee Kennedy (Virginia)

¾ lb. dried beef
6 strips lean bacon
6 chicken breasts, boned
1 (10½ oz.) can condensed mushroom soup

CHICKEN CORDON BLEU (Serves 8)

Skin and bone chicken breasts; halve lengthwise. Place chicken between two pieces of plastic wrap. Pound chicken until ⅛

4 large chicken breasts
1 pkg. boiled ham
1 pkg. Swiss cheese
1 beaten egg

inch thick; peel off wrap. Using ½ piece ham and ¼ piece cheese per chicken piece, place ham and cheese on chicken with about ½ inch of chicken showing all around. Roll up jellyroll fashion, tucking in ends; press to seal (may have to use toothpicks to hold in place). Coat chicken rolls with flour; dip in egg; then roll in bread crumbs. Cover; chill thoroughly. In a skillet melt butter. Brown cold chicken rolls on all sides in hot butter, about 5 minutes. Transfer to baking dish. Bake at 400° for 15-20 minutes.

–Mrs. Clay Corvin (Carol)

¼ c. bread crumbs
¼ c. butter
¼ c. all-purpose flour

CREAMY CHICKEN CASSEROLE (Serves 4)

Put chicken in bottom of casserole dish. Mix together soup, chicken broth, and sour cream; stir in cooked noodles and pour whole mixture over chicken in casserole. Crumble Ritz crackers over top. Bake in 350° oven for 15 minutes. Take out and put grated cheese over top. Put back in oven to let cheese melt, about 5 minutes. *–Mrs. Terry Sutton (Kay)*

1 boiled chicken, boned
1 can cream of chicken soup
1 c. chicken broth
1 small container sour cream
2 c. cooked noodles
Ritz crackers (about 15)
1 c. grated cheese

CHICKEN CURRY (Serves 6)

Dredge chicken in salt, pepper, and flour mixture. Brown in hot oil until golden. Remove from pan; drain all but 2 tablespoons of oil. Add onion, bell pepper, and curry; sauté. Return chicken to pan; pour tomatoes on top. Add water if needed; simmer 45 minutes. Serve on fluffy white rice.

–Mrs. Thomas Moody (Melba)

1 frying chicken
salt and pepper
flour
1 medium onion, minced
1 medium bell pepper, chopped
2-4 t. curry powder
1 large can whole tomatoes or 2 c. fresh or frozen tomatoes

CHICKEN CURRY (Serves 8)

Skin chicken. Cook until it falls off the bone. Remove chicken and cut into bite-sized pieces. Place chicken in shallow baking dish and cover with cooked broccoli.

Mix mayonnaise, soup, lemon juice, and

2 whole chicken breasts
6 chicken thighs
2 pkgs. broccoli flowerets
2 cans cream of chicken soup
¾ c. mayonnaise
2 t. lemon juice
1 t. powered curry

curry powder and pour over broccoli chicken. Pour melted oleo on top. Sprinkle herb dressing on top. Bake 30 minutes in 350° oven. This dish may be made ahead and kept frozen until ready to bake.

–Mrs. James Richardson

½ stick melted oleo
¾ pkg. Pepperidge Farm herb dressing

MISSIONARY CURRY (Serves 12)

Cut up chicken; add salt; and cover with water. Boil until tender; reserve chicken stock. Remove chicken from bones and cut into cubes. Heat oil in deep saucepan; add chopped onion, sauté until tender but not brown; add chopped chicken, celery salt, and curry powder; sauté; add chicken stock. Bring to rolling boil, add thickening (flour and water), stirring constantly. Lower heat and allow to simmer 15 minutes. Serve over hot boiled rice. Have as many condiments as desired. Each person chooses from the following, and after he is served, sprinkles these on top: chopped celery, chopped nuts, chopped pineapple, raisins, coconut, chopped onion, chopped crisp bacon, and chutney (if available).

–Mrs. Thomas J. DeLaughter (Lurlean)

1 hen or large stewing chicken
2 t. curry powder
1 t. salt
½ t. celery salt
½ c. onion, chopped
3 T. oil or shortening
chicken stock
condiments

AMIABLE CHICKEN CURRY (with Sambals) (Serves 6)

This is a nice cooperative curry that will wait for hours, if it has to, in the top of a double boiler, and it's easy to double. Moreover, you don't have to stew a whole chicken to get the meat. The 1½ tablespoons of curry powder listed here are enough for most people, but if you're exceptionally curry-minded, add another tablespoon. Simmer the chicken in about 1-1½ cup water until it's tender. Remove the meat and chunk it, but don't throw out the broth. Now melt the butter; add the curry powder, chop-

4 whole chicken breasts
4 T. butter
1½ T. curry powder
1 apple, chopped
1 onion, chopped
2 cans cream of chicken soup

ped apple, and onion; and sauté 15 minutes. Then stir in the undiluted soup, thinning it with the chicken broth and a little milk if you need it, until it's a good sauce consistency. Add the chicken and keep the entire mixture hot in the top of your double boiler.

Sambals

Use three or four of any of these, depending on how much you feel like chopping and how many little dishes you have. TIP: Sprinkle lemon juice on bananas to prevent their discoloring. Don't be afraid to try this. Encourage guests to pile on sambals.

–Missions Committee, N.O.B.T.S.

chopped peanuts
chopped green onions
sliced bananas
coconut
chopped crisp bacon
chopped cucumber
raisins
chutney

CHICKEN ALMANDINE (Serves 8)

Put butter in frying pan. Rub chicken breasts with salt, pepper, and paprika. Brown well on both sides. Put in baking dish with lid. Add 4 level tablespoons flour to melted butter, 2 cups water, and 2 cans mushrooms with juice (or use one can condensed cream of mushroom soup and 1 can mushrooms). Pour this over chicken. Cook about 1¾ hours at 300°. Just before serving add 1 cup of cream or Pet milk and sprinkle with 1 package toasted sliced almonds. Good served over rice.

–Mrs. Tony Hendrix (Marie)

2 sticks oleo
8 chicken breasts

CHICKEN SPAGHETTI (Serves 8)

Cook spaghetti in boiling salted water until tender. Arrange spaghetti and chicken in alternate layers in a 3-quart casserole. Brown celery, onion, and pepper in a little butter for 10 minutes. Add soups and water and cook 5 minutes longer. Pour sauce over chicken and

1 (8 oz.) pkg. spaghetti
2 c. cooked chicken
½ c. celery, diced
1 medium-sized onion, sliced
½ c. green pepper, diced
1 can condensed cream of mushroom soup

spaghetti, mix, and heat; sprinkle with cheese and bake in a 350° oven.

–The Committee

1 can condensed Cheddar cheese soup
1 can tomato soup

CAROLINA CHICKEN CASSEROLE (Serves 4-6)

Mix all ingredients in a large casserole. Cover with 1 cup crushed cornflakes. Bake in 325° oven for 1 hour.

–Mrs. Bob Neil (Judy)

2 c. cooked chicken
1 c. cream of chicken soup
1½ c. cooked rice
1 c. chopped celery
½ t. salt
½ c. slivered almonds
½ c. of broth
1 c. of mayonnaise
1 t. lemon juice
1 t. onion
2 chopped boiled eggs
½ c. water chestnuts

CHICKEN NUT CASSEROLE (Serves 4)

Cook and bone chicken. Set aside ½ cup noodles. Combine all ingredients except nuts. Place in casserole and sprinkle nuts and noodles on top. Bake at 350° for 30 minutes.

–Mary Jo Patterson

1 chicken
1 c. (3 oz.) chow mein noodles
½ can of water
¼ c. minced onions
2 cans cream of chicken soup
1½ c. chopped celery
3 eggs, hard-cooked and sliced
salt and pepper to taste
¼ c. almonds or ¼ c. salted peanuts

CHINESE CHICKEN CASSEROLE (Serves 8-10)

Combine chicken, rice, and celery (all cooked). Add soup, mayonnaise, onion, water chestnuts. Put in large uncovered casserole. Top with cornflakes mixed with margarine and almonds. Bake at 350° for 45 minutes. (May be prepared ahead and frozen.)

–Mrs. Lawrence Goff (Linda)

3-4 c. cooked chicken (2 large broilers)
1 c. uncooked rice
1 c. celery, boiled
1½ cans cream of chicken soup
¾-1 c. mayonnaise
2 t. onions
1 (8 oz.) can water chestnuts
1 c. cornflake crumbs
½ stick oleo
½ c. slivered almonds

CHEESE-CHICKEN CASSEROLE (Serves 15)

Cook, cool, cut chicken bite-sized. Put all ingredients in chicken stock to boil except peas and chicken. Add these after 15 minutes of cooking. Pour in casserole, cover with buttered bread crumbs. (Freezes beautifully.) Bake at 350° for 30 minutes.

–Mrs. Russell McIntire (Maellen)

2 fryers
1 bell pepper, chopped
1 onion, chopped
7 stems celery, chopped
2 cans cream of mushroom soup
1 small (2 oz.) pimentos
2 pkg. medium width noodles
½ lb. mild Cheddar cheese
1 large can English peas, drained

COMPANY CHICKEN CASSEROLE (Serves 10)

Mix all ingredients except bread crumbs and butter. Place mixture in buttered casserole dish. Lightly brown bread crumbs in butter and sprinkle on top. Refrigerate over night. Take out of refrigerator one hour before baking. Bake in 350° oven for 45-50 minutes.

–Mrs. Thomas J. DeLaughter (Lurlean)

2 c. chopped cooked chicken
4 hard-boiled eggs
2 c. cooked rice
1½ c. chopped celery
1 small onion, chopped
1 c. mayonnaise
2 cans cream of mushroom soup
1 (3 oz.) pkg. slivered almonds
1 t. salt
2 T. lemon juice
1 c. bread crumbs
2 T. butter

CHICKEN AND ASPARAGUS CASSEROLE (Serves 4)

Boil chicken breasts until done. Bone meat and cut up. Grease a large casserole pan. Drain asparagus. Mix soup, lemon juice, and mayonnaise. Layer chicken, asparagus, and cheese. Pour mixture over layered ingredients. Top with grated cheese. Bake in 350° oven for 40 minutes.

–Mrs. Robert Neese (Beth)

3 or 4 chicken breasts
2 cans asparagus
2 cans cream of chicken soup
1 T. lemon juice
Cheddar cheese, as desired
1 c. mayonnaise

CHICKEN-ASPARAGUS CASSEROLE (Serves 6-8)

Place the above ingredients in layers in a casserole dish in the following order: chicken, asparagus, pimento, soup, almonds. Bake at 350° for 25 minutes.

–Mrs. Joe B. Nesom (Janice)

3 cans asparagus
2 cans cream of mushroom soup
8 chicken breasts (boiled) cut in bite-sized pieces
1 small jar pimentos
1 pkg. slivered almonds

CHICKEN AND GRAVY QUICKLY (Serves 4)

Cover chicken pieces with flour. Brown in hot oil until chicken is cooked through. Add can of chicken or mushroom soup or both. Simmer for 45 minutes. *–Mrs. Earl Taylor*

4-6 pieces of chicken
1 can cream of chicken soup
1 can cream of mushroom soup (optional)

CHICKEN PARMESAN (Serves 6)

Skin desired number of chicken breasts. Dip breasts in melted margarine; roll in crushed saltines; sprinkle with garlic salt, Parmesan cheese, and parsley flakes. Place in oblong pyrex pan. Bake slowly at 275° for 1½-2 hours. *–Mrs. Bill Rogers (Lowilda)*

6 chicken breasts
1 stick margarine
20 or more saltines, crushed
¼ t. garlic salt
½ c. Parmesan cheese
2 T. parsley flakes

FIVE-MINUTE CHINESE CHICKEN (Serves 4)

In a large skillet, heat peanut oil. When oil is hot, add chicken, scallions, celery, carrot, and cabbage. Cook over medium-high temperature about 1-2 minutes. Pour chicken broth in center of mixture; cover and steam one minute. Dissolve cornstarch in water. Add cornstarch and soy sauce, toss chicken and vegetables to allow thickened sauce to cover all ingredients. Serve immediately over chow mein noodles. (Sliced water chestnuts may be added for extra crunch and flavor.) NOTE: This is a great recipe for dieters. *–The Committee*

1 T. peanut oil
1-2 c. chicken, cooked and diced
3 scallions, chopped
1 celery stalk, diced
1 carrot, thinly sliced
2½ c. cabbage, shredded
½ c. chicken broth
1 T. cornstarch
¼ c. water
2 T. soy sauce
5 oz. Chinese chow mein noodles
5-6 water chestnuts, sliced, optional

GOURMET BAKED CHICKEN WITH EGG NOODLES (Serves 4)

Brown chicken in fat in heavy skillet. Boil noodles about 6 minutes in salted water. Drain. Melt butter in saucepan; stir in flour and salt. Add milk and bouillon cube; cook until thick, stirring constantly. Add pimento, mushrooms, and green pepper. Fold in noodles. Pour into greased 1½-quart casserole. Arrange fried chicken on top.

4 servings chicken
¼ c. fat
5 oz. egg noodles
1 T. butter or margarine
2 T. enriched flour
½ t. salt
1¼ c. milk
1 bouillon cube
¼ c. chopped pimento
1 small can mushrooms, sliced
¼ green pepper, chopped

Gourmet Sauce:

Pour half of sauce over chicken. Bake at 450° for 20 minutes. Then pour remaining sauce over chicken and continue baking at 250° about 15 minutes, or until chicken is tender. NOTE: If you can buy green, or spinach noodles, use them; for this makes a colorful, easy and delicious dish.

–The Committee

¼ c. melted butter or margarine
1 t. vinegar
¼ t. paprika
1 t. prepared mustard
½ t. salt

HOT CHICKEN SALAD (Serves 8)

Combine all of the above. Let stand in refrigerator overnight. Top with: 1 cup grated cheese, 1 cup potato chips, ⅔ cups finely cut toasted, almonds. Bake at 400°.

–Mrs. Billy Simmons (Flo)

4 c. cooked chopped chicken
2 T. lemon juice
¾ cup mayonnaise
1 t. salt
2 cups chopped celery
4 hard-cooked eggs, sliced
¾ c. cream of chicken soup, condensed
1 t. finely grated onion
2 pimentos, cut fine

NO-PEEK CHICKEN (Serves 6)

Line shallow baking dish with foil; leave about 8 inches extra on each side. Mix rice, creamed soups, and milk. Pour into lined dish. Top with chicken. Sprinkle with dry soup mix. Seal foil tightly. Bake at 325° for 2½ hours. Do not open foil until ready to serve.

–Mrs. Paul M. Hugger (Vickie)

1½ c. Minute rice
1 can cream of mushroom soup
1 can cream of celery soup
½ c. milk
1 pkg. dry onion soup mix
6 chicken breasts

POLYNESIAN CHICKEN BREASTS (Serves 4-6)

Stir together in 2-cup measuring cup cinnamon, curry powder, garlic salt, and honey. Mix well. Then add grapefruit juice and mix well. Put a little sauce into pan just to cover bottom.

Place halved chicken breasts in pan, skin side down. Pour remaining sauce over chicken and cover. Simmer 20 minutes over low

4-6 chicken breasts, halved
1 T. cinnamon
1½ t. curry powder
1½ t. garlic salt
½ c. honey
¾ c. grapefruit juice
1 c. (8 oz.) crushed pineapple
1 T. cornstarch

heat or until tender (can be left to simmer longer). Remove chicken from pan and place skin side upon broiler rack. Remove skin if desired; I like to leave it on. Add pineapple and juice to pan. Heat and stir until starting to boil, add cornstarch mixed with 2 tablespoons water to sauce and pineapple. Stir and mix well. Spoon thickened sauce over chicken and place under broiler 4-6 inches from heat for 5 minutes or until glazed lightly. Sauce makes delicious gravy over rice or noodles.

–Mrs. Joseph Borgkvist (Jo Ann)

CHICKEN-RICE CASSEROLE (Serves 8)

1 pkg. instant chicken broth (or 1 chicken bouillon cube)
1½ c. boiling water
1 c. rice
1 smell can boned chicken
1 can mushrooms (sliced)
1 can water chestnuts, sliced
1 can cream of onion soup
¾ stick butter
salt, pepper, parsley

Mix bouillon and hot water. Pour over rice. Add chicken (drained), water chestnuts, and mushrooms, onion soup (cream of mushroom may be used—eliminate use of can of mushrooms). Salt and pepper to taste, dab with parsley. Add half of butter. Stir well. Pour into large casserole dish. Bake at 350°. Cover dish first 30 minutes; uncover. Stir well and add remaining butter. Leave uncovered and cook 30 minutes longer.

–Mrs. James Taylor (Maidee)

SURPRISE CHICKEN (Serves 4-6)

Soak chicken in Italian dressing overnight—dry a little. Roll in Ritz cracker crumbs. Bake at 350° for one hour. This is easy to prepare and has a very unusual flavor. *–The Committee*

CURRIED CHICKEN CUPS (Serves 4)

2 pkg. broccoli spears, cooked
1 chicken cooked and boned
1 can cream of chicken soup
1 c. mayonnaise
1 t. lemon juice

Place cooked broccoli spears in casserole dish. Combine remaining ingredients and spread on top of broccoli. Top with cheese. Bake at 350° for 30 minutes. Spoon into baked pastry shells. Serve at once. For variation, serve over rice instead of in patty shells. *–Mrs. Tom Monroe (Simone)*

¼ curry powder
½ c. sharp Cheddar

BROCCOLI AND CHICKEN CASSEROLE (Serves 6)

Boil chicken breasts until tender. Remove from bone. Cook broccoli according to package directions. Place in bottom of 3-quart pyrex dish. Then add chicken, which has been broken into bite-sized pieces. Mix soup, cheese, mayonnaise, and lemon pepper well and pour over chicken and broccoli. Heat until bubbly hot. *–Mrs. John F. Gibson*

6 chicken breasts
1 (10 oz.) pkg. frozen, chopped broccoli
3 cans cream of chicken soup
2 c. sharp grated cheese
2 T. mayonnaise
2 heaping t. lemon pepper (do not omit this)

CORN BREAD DRESSING

Put in a small pan and cover with water; bring to a boil. Let simmer for 10 minutes. Set aside.

1 c. finely chopped celery
1-2 onions, chopped

Mix all together. Add celery and onions with the simmered water to corn bread mixture. If not moist enough, add chicken broth or turkey broth until moist. Can add butter if it needs a richer taste. Put in a pan and bake at about 400° until slightly brown on top. *–Mrs. Paul Earley (Jackie)*

1 small pan crumbled corn bread
6 boiled eggs, crumbled with hands
sage to taste
½ stack saltine crackers, crumbled
salt and pepper to taste

BEEF ORIENTAL (Serves 4)

Brown onion and celery in butter. Remove from pan. Brown rice and ground beef. Put aside. In buttered 1-quart casserole, combine soups, water, soy sauce, and pepper. Add brown onion, celery, ground beef, and rice. Stir in bean sprouts lightly. Cover and bake in moderate 350° oven. Serve with Chinese noodles. *–Mrs. Wayne Hoggle (Romie)*

2 onions
1 c. sliced celery
3 T. butter
½ c. rice, uncooked
1 lb. ground beef
1 can cream of chicken soup
1 can Chinese noodles
1 can cream of mushroom soup
1 c. water
¼ c. soy sauce
¼ t. pepper
1 can bean sprouts

BEEF STROGANOFF (Serves 6)

Cut meat into strips. Melt butter in skillet. Brown meat, add mushrooms. Add bouillon and water. Simmer until bouillon is dissolved. Pour ⅔ cup broth into mixing bowl and add flour. To meat add onion, catsup, and garlic salt. Simmer 15 minutes. Add sour cream. Mix thoroughly. Add 7-Up just before serving. Heat through; serve over noodles. *–Mrs. Steve Wallace (Janet)*

1½ lb. round steak
½ c. margarine
1 can mushrooms, sliced
2 beef bouillon cubes
2½ c. water
⅓ c. onion
2 T. catsup
dash garlic salt
⅓ c. flour
8-oz. carton sour cream
¾ c. 7-Up

POOR MAN'S BEEF STROGANOFF (Serves 4-6)

Brown meat and onions. Add rest of ingredients. Put in casserole and top with bread crumbs. Bake at 350° for 30 minutes.

–Mrs. Fred B. Moseley (Gay)

1½ lb. ground beef
1 c. onion, chopped
1 c. whole kernel corn, drained
3 c. noodles, cooked
1 c. bread crumbs
1 c. sour cream
¼ c. pimento, chopped
salt and pepper
1 can cream of mushroom soup
1 can cream of chicken soup

BRASELLI HAMBURGERS (Serves 2-4)

Melt margarine in skillet; cook onion until tender. Mix other ingredients in a bowl. Form meat mixture into patties. Brown patties in margarine and onion (cover); turn and brown on other side. Takes approximately 30 minutes.

–Mrs. Cecil Braselli (Candy)

3 T. margarine
1 small onion sliced
1 lb. ground beef
1 egg
salt and pepper to taste
2 small handfuls crushed potato chips
2 good shakes Worcestershire sauce

CHEESEBURGER CASSEROLE (Serves 4-6)

Combine meat and onion in skillet. Cook until meat is lightly browned. Drain; add salt and pepper. Stir in catsup and tomato sauce. Put half this mixture in 1½-quart casserole; place half the cheese on top; then add remaining meat mixture, covering with rest of cheese. Top with biscuits and bake at

1 lb. ground beef
½ c. chopped onion
¾ t. salt
⅛ t. pepper
¾ c. catsup
1 (8 oz.) can tomato sauce
1 (8 oz.) pkg. American cheese slices
1 can refrigerator biscuits

425° for 20-25 minutes, or until biscuits are golden brown.

–Mrs. Morris Murray (Brenda)
Mrs. Dennis Rogers (Judy)

CORN BREAD PIE (Serves 6-8)

1 lb. ground beef
1 large onion
1 can tomato soup
2 c. water
1 t. salt
¾ t. black pepper
1 T. chili powder
½ c. green pepper
1 c. whole kernel corn, drained

Brown beef and onion in skillet; add soup, water, seasoning, corn, and green pepper. Mix well; simmer 18 minutes. Then fill a greased casserole dish three-quarters full. Leave room for corn bread topping.

Topping:

¾ c. corn meal
1 T. flour
1 T. sugar
½ t. salt
1½ t. baking powder

Sift together. Add 1 beaten egg, ½-cup milk, 1 tablespoon melted fat. Cover the meat mixture with the corn bread topping. Bake at 350° 20 minutes or until bread is done.

–Mrs. Wayne Hoggle (Romie)

GROUND BEEF SUPREME (Serves 6)

1 lb. ground beef
½ c. chopped celery
⅓ c. chopped onion
salt and pepper
3 c. Pepperidge Farm Dressing
1 c. water
1 stick margarine
1 (10½ oz.) can cream of celery (or mushroom) soup
½ c. Parmesan cheese

Sauté ingredients in frying pan until meat loses its red color (no need to brown). Divide meat mixture in half. Place half the meat in pyrex dish (greased). Spread mixture in layer over bottom of dish.

Mix dressing with water and margarine. Spread all of this over first layer. Then spread second half of meat mixture over dressing mixture.

Cover with can of undiluted cream of celery or mushroom soup. Sprinkle generously with Parmesan cheese and bake at 350° for 35 minutes or until light brown.

–Mrs. Raymond Garner (Donna)

HAMBURGER-MACARONI BAKE (Serves 6)

Prepare macaroni and cheese dinner according to package directions. Meanwhile, brown ground beef; spoon off excess fat. Remove from heat; stir in Manwich, soup, and prepared macaroni and cheese. Turn into 2-quart casserole; sprinkle with cracker crumbs.

Bake uncovered in 350° oven for 35 minutes. (I usually make two 1-quart casseroles and freeze one. Leave crumbs off of one and add them when it is baked.)

–Mrs. James Gallery (Debra)

1 (7¼ oz.) pkg. macaroni and cheese dinner mix
1 lb. ground beef
1 (15½ oz.) can original flavor Manwich sandwich sauce
1 can condensed golden mushroom soup
⅓ c. coarsely crushed Ritz crackers

HOME-STYLE ROUND STEAK (Serves 6)

Cut steak into serving pieces; coat with flour. In an ovenproof skillet, brown meat in hot oil. Season with salt and pepper. Add 1 cup water, bouillon cube, parsley, sugar, and thyme. Cover and bake at 350° until tender (1½ to 2 hours); remove beef. Measure pan juices; add enough water to equal 1½ cups. Combine with flour and Kitchen Bouquet. Cook until thick and bubbly. Serve gravy over meat. *–Mrs. Julian Stephens (Tamara)*

1½ lb. beef round
2 T. flour
2 T. oil
1 c. water
1 beef bouillon cube
2 T. parsley, chopped
1 t. sugar
½ t. thyme leaves
½ t. Kitchen Bouquet
3 T. flour

ISLANDER BEEF SHORT RIBS (Serves 6)

Place short ribs in large fry pan or Dutch oven; cover tightly and cook slowly 1½ hours. Pour off drippings; season meat with 1 teaspoon salt. Combine pineapple and liquid, onion, catsup, vinegar, water, green pepper, brown sugar, mustard, and ½-teaspoon salt. Pour mixture over short ribs, cover tightly and continue cooking 30 minutes or until meat is tender. Put meat on platter. Thicken sauce with cornstarch and water and serve.

–Mrs. Joseph Borgkvist (Jo Ann)

3-4 lb. beef short ribs
1 t. salt
1 (15¾ oz.) can pineapple tidbits
½ c. finely chopped onion
½ c. catsup
½ c. vinegar
½ c. water
½ c. chopped green pepper
3 T. brown sugar
½ t. dry mustard
½ t. salt
1 T. cornstarch in ½ c. water

MEATLOAF (Serves 4-6)

Mix all ingredients together. Use bread crumbs as needed to provide good texture. Form into loaf and cover top with catsup. Bake uncovered at 375° for 45-60 minutes.

–Mrs. Ray Davidson (Virginia)

2 lb. ground beef
1 pkg. onion soup mix
2 eggs
1 can tomatoes, drained
1½ c. bread crumbs
salt and pepper to taste

MEATBALLS IN SWEET AND SOUR SAUCE (Serves 4)

Combine beef with next 7 ingredients. Mix well and shape into 12 balls. Sprinkle lightly with flour, and brown meatballs on all sides in bacon or other fat.

Mix packaged sweet and sour sauce according to directions, but *do not heat*. Add tomato sauce to sweet and sour mixture. Arrange meatballs and vegetables in 2½-quart casserole. Pour sauce over. Cover and bake at 350° for 1 hour. If you have a crockpot, cook on low for about 8 hours.

–Mrs. Charles Westbrook (Jane)

1 lb. ground chuck beef
2 T. chopped onion
2 T. chopped green pepper
¼ c. corn meal
1 t. salt
1 t. chili powder
1 egg
⅓-½ c. catsup
1 pkg. sweet and sour mix
1 (8 oz.) can tomato sauce
4 potatoes, peeled and quartered
4 carrots, scraped and halved

RAPID ROAST (Serves 8)

Preheat oven to 500°. Rub roast with garlic and sprinkle with salt. Place roast in preheated oven. Roast for 30 minutes and then turn heat off. Do not open the door for exactly two hours. Then open it and remove the roast. Allow the roast to stand 15 minutes before carving. If you wish more well-done meat, roast 33 or 34 minutes in 500° oven before turning the heat off.

–The Committee

4-6-lb. beef roast (prime rib, boneless rump, boneless sirloin)
1 clove garlic

MAKE-IT-NOW, BAKE-IT-LATER COMPANY ROAST

In mid-afternoon (after lunch), place seasoned beef in uncovered roasting pan in 375° preheated oven. After 1 hour, turn off the oven. Do not open oven door at all. Before serving time: for rare roast beef, turn oven to

1 standing rib roast, any size
salt and pepper

300° and leave for 45 minutes; for medium beef, 50 minutes at 300°, for medium well done, 55 minutes at 300°. Don't peek! Let stand 20 minutes before cutting.

–The Committee

OVEN-BARBECUED BEEF ROAST (Serves 7)

Brown or sear both sides of meat in oil. Cover with water and cook for 2½ hours over medium heat. Salt after it has cooked a while. Remove from heat and squeeze the juice of one lemon over the surface of the roast. Mix 1 teaspoon liquid smoke with ⅓ cup barbecue sauce. Brush on meat with pastry brush. Bake in oven at 325-350° for 2½-3 hours. Leave about 1 inch of water in the bottom all the time the meat is roasting. If it needs to cook longer to be tender, lower the heat. Keep roaster covered until the last 30 minutes.

–Mrs. George Harrison (Jean)

4 lb. chuck roast
1 T. oil
1 lemon
1 t. liquid smoke
⅓ c. barbecue sauce

ROULADEN (GERMAN-STYLE ROLLED STEAK) (Serves 6)

Spread each piece of steak with salt, pepper, and mustard. Place a piece of bacon, a ¼-inch slice of pickle, onions, and parsley down into the center and roll the meat around it. Tie the rolls with cord; or use toothpicks or skewers. Melt fat in skillet; add beef rolls and brown them in hot fat on all sides. Add water if needed. Cook meat until tender. (Can also be baked in 300° oven for about 1½ hours or cooked in electric skillet, all-day cooker, or pressure cooker, following manufacturer's suggestions.) Remove meat from skillet and save liquid. Melt butter in saucepan and sprinkle in the flour. Cook until flour is browned. Gradually add the cooking liquid (a bouillon cube may be

6 top round steak pieces, sliced ¼-inch thick (or 1½ lb. beef round steak)
1 t. salt
pepper
6 t. mustard
6 slices lean bacon
3 dill pickle slices
½ c. chopped onion
parsley
3 T. fat
1 T. butter
2 T. flour
2 c. water

used). Cook until thick. Taste for seasoning and return rouladen to the skillet. Simmer over low heat long enough to heat the rolls.

–Mrs. Carl Mueller (Mary)

PORCUPINE MEATBALLS I (Serves 6)

Mix ¼-cup soup, meat, rice, egg, onion, and salt. Shape into 16 meatballs. Brown in shortening. Blend remaining soup and water; pour over browned meatballs. Cover and simmer about 40 minutes or until rice is tender. Serve hot.

–Mrs. George Tumlin (Lynda)

1 can tomato soup
1 lb. ground beef
¼ c. raw rice
1 egg, slightly beaten
¼ c. onion, minced
1 t. salt
2 T. shortening
1 c. water

PORCUPINE MEATBALLS II (Serves 4)

Combine rice, onions, and ground beef and season as desired. Make into medium-sized meatballs. Pour tomato soup (or sauce) into pressure cooker. Season as desired. Drop meatballs into sauce. Cook under pressure of 15 pounds for 15 to 20 minutes or as needed with your pressure cooker.

–Mrs. Paul Frazer (Marilyn)

⅓ c. regular rice
½ c. finely chopped onion
1 lb. lean ground beef
garlic powder
salt
pepper
Worcestershire sauce
1 can tomato soup or sauce

TEXAS CASSEROLE (Serves 4)

Chop onions and brown. Add meat. Salt and pepper to taste. Add herb sauce and sugar. Simmer-boil noodles. Mash soft cream cheese and sour cream. Layer first noodles then meat then cream cheese and top with American cheese slices. Makes two medium-sized casseroles, one to eat and one to freeze. When taken from the freezer, bake at 375° for 45 minutes.

–Mrs. Ron McCaskill (Fran)

1 medium onion, chopped
1 lb. ground beef
1 can herb tomato sauce
2 t. sugar
1 pkg. elbow noodles
8 oz. cream cheese
4 oz. sour cream

TEXAS HASH (Serves 6)

Brown in fat on medium heat:

3 T. shortening
2 onions, chopped
2 green peppers, chopped
1 lb. ground beef (or ¾ lb. ground beef and ½ lb. sausage)

Rice mixture:

Wash and add rice. Cover with tomatoes. Season with chili powder, salt, and pepper. Turn range to high until steaming, then turn to very low for 30 minutes (or bake covered for 45 minutes in 350° oven; remove cover and bake 15 minutes longer).

–Mrs. Ron McCaskill (Fran)

½ c. rice
2 c. canned tomatoes
1 t. chili powder
1 t. salt
¼ t. pepper

WESTERN-STYLE HASH (Serves 4-6)

Brown beef in skillet. Add remaining ingredients. Simmer 15 minutes, stirring occasionally. Top with thin slices of cheese of own choice. May be served with corn chips and salad. *–George T. Flanagan*

3 lb. ground beef
1 can whole kernel corn with juice
1 small jar of spaghetti sauce
1 large can pork and beans

LASAGNA I (Serves 4-6)

Brown beef, onion, celery, and garlic; add salt, pepper, parsley, and oregano. Add tomato paste and sauce; stir in hot water. Mix well. Simmer sauce 15 minutes. Cook noodles while sauce simmers. Layer as follows: meat / noodles / meat / cheeses / noodles / meat / cheeses. Bake 45-60 minutes in 350° oven. *–Mrs. Clay Corvin (Carol)*

1½ lb. ground beef
1 medium onion, chopped
1 rib celery, chopped (about ¼ c.)
1 clove garlic or garlic powder
1 t. salt
¼ t. pepper
1 t. parsley
½ t. oregano
1 (12 oz.) can tomato paste
1 (6 oz.) can tomato sauce
1½ c. hot water
lasagna noodles (about 7)
½ carton (8 oz.) cottage cheese
8 oz. Mozzarella, grated
Parmesan cheese

LASAGNA II (Serves 6)

Cook ground meat; add parsley flakes, salt and pepper, and spaghetti sauce. Cook and drain lasagna noodles. Beat eggs and mix with Ricotta, Mozzarella, and Parmesan cheeses. Layer noodles, cheeses, and meat sauce. Cook at 350° until bubbly.

–Mrs. Edgar Graves (Marilyn)

2 lb. ground beef
1 T. parsley flakes
salt and pepper
3 (15½ oz.) jars spaghetti sauce
1 lb. lasagna noodles, cooked
2 beaten eggs
1 lb. Ricotta cheese
1 lb. Mozzarella cheese
1 c. Parmesan cheese

SPAGHETTI SAUCE I (Serves 8)

Brown meat, onion, bell pepper, and celery. Stir in remaining ingredients. Bring to a boil. Cover. Simmer 1 hour. Stir occasionally. Uncover and simmer 15-30 minutes. Serve over spaghetti. Can be prepared in advance and frozen. *–Mrs. Tom Mills (Leslie)*

2 lb. ground round
1 onion
1 bell pepper
2 stalks celery
1 large can stewed tomatoes
1 (6 oz.) can tomato sauce
3 c. water
1 T. sugar
1 t. oregano
1 t. pepper

SPAGHETTI SAUCE II (Serves 6-8)

Sauté beef, onion, and garlic. Add other ingredients. Simmer over low heat 2 hours, stirring occasionally. Serve over spaghetti.
–Miss Sandi Swartz

1½ lb. ground beef
1 c. chopped onion or 4 T. instant minced onion
4 t. basil
5 T. instant parsley
4 t. salt
2 cloves garlic
2-lb. can tomatoes, sieved
1-lb. can tomato sauce
1 (6 oz.) can tomato paste
1 t. pepper
2 dashes cayenne
2 t. oregano
½ c. water

GERMAN SPAGHETTI SAUCE (Serves 4)

Brown the meat, crumbling as you brown. Sauté the onions and celery in bacon drippings, and with the other ingredients, add to the meat and simmer for at least 4 hours.
–William F. Morgan

1 lb. ground chuck
¼ c. chopped onion
½ c. chopped celery
¼ c. bacon drippings
2 cloves garlic (finely chopped)
canned whole tomatoes (3-4 cups)
1 can tomato paste
½ t. paprika
¼ t. black pepper
1 small can mushrooms
1 can tomato sauce
2 t. salt
small piece bay leaf
dash of cayenne

MANICOTTI (Serves 6)

Combine eggs, flour, milk, oil, and beat until smooth. It should look like pancake batter. Place ⅛ cup on hot, slightly greased, 7-inch skillet and cook only until crepe is set; turn over and cook only slightly. Stack pancakes, separating them each with waxed paper.

1 c. slightly beaten eggs
1 c. milk
1 c. all-purpose flour
1 T. salad oil

Filling:

Mix thoroughly. Set aside. Before you begin the manicotti you should have ready a large quantity of Italian spaghetti sauce and meatballs. Now assemble the casserole. Stuff crepes with filling and roll up like enchiladas. Put layer of tomato sauce in large rectangular pan. Lay Ricotta rolls in a single layer. Cover with sauce and make a second layer. Cover all with tomato sauce and meat balls. Bake at 350° until the manicotti puff up, about 30-40 minutes.

–Mrs. James Mosteller (Iris)

2-3 lbs. Ricotta cheese
2-3 eggs
chopped parsley
Parmesan cheese (½ c.)

ITALIAN CASSEROLE (Serves 6)

In skillet, brown meat with onion, garlic, and seasonings. Stir to separate. Combine in 1½-quart casserole meat, soup, water, and noodles. Place grated cheese on top. Bake at 350° for 30 minutes.

–Mrs. Leroy Yarbrough (Edwyna)

1 lb. ground beef
½ c. chopped onion
1 medium clove garlic, minced
½-1 t. oregano
½ t. salt
1 can tomato soup
⅓ c. water
2 c. cooked noodles
1 c. grated Cheddar cheese

PIZZA BY THE YARD (Serves 4-5)

Cut loaf in half lengthwise. Combine tomato paste, Parmesan cheese, onion, oregano, salt, and ⅛ t. pepper. Add meat; mix well. Spread atop loaf halves. Place on baking sheet. Bake at 400° for 20 minutes. Remove from oven; top with tomato slices and green pepper rings. Sprinkle cheese over tomatoes. Bake for 5 minutes.

–Mrs. David Sandifer (Jackie)

1 unsliced loaf French bread
1 (6 oz.) can tomato paste
⅓ c. grated Parmesan cheese
¼ c. finely chopped green onion
½ t. dried oregano, crushed
¾ t. salt
1 lb. ground beef
2 tomatoes, sliced
1 green pepper, cut in rings
4 oz. sharp processed American cheese, shredded

ITALIAN STUFFED PASTA WITH WHEAT GERM (Serves 4)

Cook manicotti in boiling salted water as package directs. Drain and rinse with cold water. Meanwhile, sauté onion in butter until limp and light golden. Mix in garlic powder and tomato sauce. Brown beef. Remove from heat and mix in toasted wheat germ, Parmesan cheese, oregano, basil, salt, pepper, and ¾ cup of tomato mixture. Stuff into manicotti. Pour half of remaining sauce into baking dish. Place manicotti in sauce in single layer. Top with Monterey Jack cheese slices, covering completely. Pour remaining sauce around outside edge. Cover. Bake in 425° oven for 25 minutes or until heated through. Sprinkle top with minced parsley.

–The Committee

8 manicotti shells
½ c. chopped onions
2 T. butter
⅛ t. garlic powder
2 cans tomato sauce (15 oz.)
1 lb. ground beef
⅔ c. toasted wheat germ
¼ c. grated Parmesan cheese
1 t. oregano, crushed
½ t. basil, crushed
½ t. salt
¼ t. pepper
Monterey Jack cheese, sliced
minced parsley

MEXICAN TORTILLAS (Serves 6)

Sift flour, baking powder and salt; cut in shortening. Add enough cold water to make rather tough dough. Pinch off balls size of large walnut; let balls stand for 15 minutes. Roll very thin on floured board. Heat skillet (iron one is best) with about ½ cup cooking oil until hot. Cook each tortilla separately 1 minute on each side or until bubbles begin to brown. You can fold tortilla while it is frying, hold in that position, and it will stay. You can freeze the uncooked balls and use at a later time. *–Mrs. Mack P. Jones (Marie)*

2 c. flour
2 t. baking powder
1 t. salt
3 T. shortening
cold water

EASY ENCHILADAS (Serves 6)

Fill each tortilla with grated cheese and onions. Roll each, securing with toothpicks. Place in pyrex dish and top with chili and enchilada sauce. Bake in 350° oven for 20 minutes. *–Mrs. Leroy Yarbrough (Edwyna)*

8 tortillas
2 c. grated Cheddar cheese
⅓ c. chopped onions (or minced)
1 large can chili (without beans)
1 small can enchilada sauce

TACOS (Serves 6)

Heat taco shells in 400° oven for 10 minutes. Cook ground beef and taco seasoning according to directions on package. Place ground beef mixture in hot taco shells. Top with lettuce and cheese. Provide piquant sauce to sprinkle on each of the tacos to add special Mexican flavor!

–Mrs. Leroy Yarbrough (Edwyna)

10 taco shells
1 lb. ground beef
½ envelope taco seasoning
chopped lettuce
grated cheese

ENCHILADA CASSEROLE

Mix all ingredients in the order shown. Break tortillas into bite-sized pieces and layer meat mixture and tortillas in a large casserole dish. Cover and bake at 325° for 45 minutes; then remove cover and bake 15 minutes longer.

–Mrs. Landrum P. Leavell (Jo Ann)

2 lbs. ground chuck
1 large onion, chopped
½ to 1 t. garlic salt
1 can cream of mushroom soup
1 can cream of chicken soup
1 can (4-5 oz.) green chili peppers, cut up
1 can enchilada sauce
½ t. chili powder
1 lb. grated Velveeta cheese
½ lb. grated sharp cheese

CHILI CON CARNE (Serves 8)

Heat fat in a large pressure cooker. Add onion, green pepper, and meat. Cook until brown, stirring occasionally. Add all other ingredients *except the beans*. Stir. Place cover on cooker and cook under pressure 15 minutes. Take off heat and let steam return to down position. Add beans if desired and heat to boiling. Serve. (If you do not wish to use a pressure cooker, just cook slowly for about 1 hour, stirring occasionally.)

–Mrs. Mack P. Jones (Marie)

3 T. bacon grease (or oil)
1 large onion, chopped
1 c. green pepper, chopped
1½-2 lb. lean ground beef
1 can (2½ c.) tomatoes
2 cans tomato sauce
1 c. sliced mushrooms
½ c. celery, chopped
1 can tomato soup
⅛-¼ t. oregano
2 T. Worcestershire sauce
3 T. vinegar
1 t. sugar
⅛ t. cayenne
1 bay leaf
2 T. chili powder (heaping for very hot)
1 clove garlic, minced
1 t. salt
1 can (2½ c.) kidney beans (optional)

FRITOS AND CHILI (Serves 6)

Grease a 2-quart casserole. Add Fritos and pour chili on top. Distribute onion over chili. Sprinkle cheese on top. Bake at 350° until cheese melts. *–The Committee*

1 (6 oz.) pkg. Fritos
2 (15 oz.) cans chili (no beans)
1 medium onion, finely chopped
1 c. grated Cheddar cheese

B-B-Q PORK CHOPS OR CHICKEN (Serves 4-6)

Combine above ingredients and pour over chops or chicken. Cover and bake at 325° for 1½ hours. *–Mrs. Tim Williams (Glennis)*

½ c. brown sugar
2 T. vinegar
½ c. catsup
3 T. mustard
1 envelope dry onion soup mix
8 pork chops or chicken pieces

BARBECUED SPARERIBS (Serves 4)

Slice ribs and cook in water with garlic cloves until well done. Marinate ribs in the following sauce at least 3 hours—best if overnight. Broil till brown, or barbecue. *–Mrs. George Harrison (Jean)*

3 lb. pork ribs
½ c. catsup
½ c. sugar
½ c. soy sauce
dash Accent
⅛ t. ground ginger
¼ t. minced garlic
dash of hot sauce (optional)
sesame seed (optional)
dash Worcestershire sauce
1 T. sherry flavoring or wine vinegar

BROCCOLI-HAM CASSEROLE (Serves 10-12)

Cut 12 doughnuts and holes from bread (easier to cut if frozen). Fit leftover bread scraps into bottom of 13-by-9-by-2-inch baking dish. Grate a layer of cheese over bread scraps. Add layer of broccoli, then ham. Arrange bread doughnuts and holes on top. Combine eggs, milk, onion, salt, and mustard and pour over casserole. Refrigerate overnight. Bake uncovered at 325° for 55 minutes. Add more shredded cheese 5 minutes before end of baking time. Let stand 10 minutes before cutting into squares and serving. *–Mrs. Tim Williams (Glennis)*

12 slices white bread
½ lb. or more sharp Cheddar
1 (10 oz.) pkg. broccoli, cooked
2 c. finely diced cooked ham
6 slightly beaten eggs
3½ c. milk
2 T. instant minced onion
½ t. salt
¼ t. dry mustard

MIRLITON AND SAUSAGE CASSEROLE (Serves 4-6)

Place whole unpeeled mirlitons in large pot and boil until tender. Cool. Peel and remove seeds. Cut into small cubes. Fry sausage and onion together until sausage is brown. Pour off grease. Add water and simmer slowly 10 minutes. Add bread crumbs (saving some for top) and mirlitons. Stir just until combined. Place in buttered casserole; top with reserved crumbs; and bake at 350° for 25-30 minutes. –*Mrs. Danny Chapman (Margaret)*

2 medium-sized mirlitons (vegetable pears)
¾ lb. ground sausage
1 medium onion, chopped
1 c. water
1 c. Italian-flavored bread crumbs
salt and pepper

SCALLOPED CORN AND SAUSAGE (Serves 4)

Brown pork sausage meat. Pour off all fat except about 2 tablespoons. Add the flour and stir until blended; then add the milk and stir until mixture boils and thickens. Add corn, salt, and pepper. Turn into a shallow casserole and arrange thick slices of tomato (2 medium) over the top. Top with grated cheese if desired. Place until broiler for 3-4 minutes to cook the tomatoes. Sprinkle with finely chopped parsley.

–*Mrs. George Herndon (Claire)*

¾ lb. pork sausage meat
3 T. flour
1¼ c. milk
1 can (1½ c.) whole kernel corn, drained
⅓ t. salt
1/16 t. pepper
2 medium tomatoes
½ c. grated cheese (optional)
1 t. parsley (if desired)

SWEET AND PUNGENT PORK (Serves 4)

Combine flour, egg, salt, and water to make a thin batter. Add pork cubes to batter and mix until well coated. Fry in hot cooking oil until nicely browned. Drain well and keep hot.

Combine green pepper strips, pineapple, brown sugar, vinegar, one cup water, and molasses. Bring to a boil, stirring constantly. Add tomatoes (cut in eighths).

Combine cornstarch and ¼ cup of water; add to hot mixture. Cook, stirring constantly, until thickened. Add pork and cook 5 minutes longer.

–*Mrs. Grady Cothen (Bettye)*

⅔ c. flour
1 egg, beaten
½ t. salt
4 T. water
1 lb. pork shoulder, ½-inch cubes
2 c. cooking oil
1 green pepper, in strips
1½ c. drained pineapple chunks
½ c. light brown sugar
¼ c. vinegar
1 c. water
2 T. molasses
1-2 small tomatoes
3 T. cornstarch
¼ c. water

FRANKFURTER CASSEROLE (Serves 6)

1 can whole tomatoes, mashed
minced onions (precooked)
1 pkg. frankfurters, sliced
2 c. cooked macaroni or noodles
1 c. grated sharp cheese

Place all ingredients in casserole dish and sprinkle with more cheese. Bake at 350° for 30 minutes. This recipe is great when you are in a hurry.

–Mrs. Raymond Garner (Donna)

Seafood

BOILED SHRIMP (Serves 4)

1 lemon
1 t. Crab boil seasoning
1 small onion
2 T. cooking oil
2 shakes hot sauce
2 garlic cloves
1 t. salt
2 qt. water
3 lb. shrimp

Bring all ingredients to boil except shrimp and cook for 5 minutes. Add shrimp. Continue to boil for 15 minutes. If small shrimp, cook 10 minutes. Let cool. Drain well. Serve with vegetable salad, French bread, iced tea, and lemon pie. *–Mrs. Ray Robbins (Louise)*

SHRIMP FOR A CROWD (Serves 10)

5 lb. salt
1 doz. lemons, cut in halves and squeezed slightly
2 bottles hot sauce
3 lb. onions, peeled and left whole
4 or 5 oz. black pepper
1 small can chili powder
3 bell peppers, sliced
20 lb. shrimp

Take a clean washtub and fill it three-quarters full of water. Add all ingredients but shrimp. Allow brew to come to a boil over a hot fire. Add shrimp; bring back to a boil; and boil for 10 minutes. Remove promptly to prevent shrimp from becoming too "hot" from the seasoning. (Whole potatoes, in their jackets, may be boiled in the brew before adding the shrimp. The onions can also be served as a side dish).

–Mrs. David Ivy (O'Hara)

SHRIMP CREOLE (Serves 6)

¾ c. chopped onion
1 c. chopped celery
4 T. butter or margarine
3 T. flour
1 T. chili powder
1 t. salt

Sauté onion and celery in butter; add flour, chili powder, salt, and water; simmer for 5 minutes; add tomatoes, sugar, vinegar, and shrimp.

Make a dish by layers of rice and shrimp

Preschool Center

sauce, or serve the rice and sauce separately.

Serves any number, depending upon amount of rice and thickness of sauce.

–Mrs. Harrison Pike (June)

1 c. water
2 c. canned tomatoes (or one can tomato sauce)
1 t. sugar
1 t. vinegar
2 c. cooked shrimp

CREOLE SHRIMP SUPREME (Serves 4)

1 large bell pepper
1 can tomatoes
1 can tomato paste
1 envelope onion soup mix
½ t. thyme
juice of ¼ lemon
dash of Worcestershire sauce
1 small bay leaf
2 lb. fresh or frozen shrimp

Brown 3 tablespoons flour in ¼ cup bacon drippings; add chopped green pepper and sauté. To this add the tomatoes, tomato paste, onion soup mix, thyme, lemon juice, Worcestershire sauce, bay leaf, and one tomato can of water. Salt and pepper to taste. Cook this mixture slowly until thickened, stirring often. Add raw shrimp and cook until shrimp are pink (about 10 or 15 minutes.) Serve over rice.

–Mrs. Eugene Patterson (Mary Jo)

SHRIMP MOLD (Makes 6 main-dish servings or about 12 for a buffet)

½ c. water
2 envelopes unflavored gelatin
1 (10¾ oz.) can condensed tomato soup
½ lb. cream cheese
½ c. finely chopped onion
½ c. finely chopped celery
1 c. finely chopped green pepper
1 c. mayonnaise
2 c. chopped, cooked shrimp

Place water in a small saucepan and sprinkle gelatin over it; let stand one minute to soften and then stir in soup. Place pan over moderate heat and stir constantly until gelatin is dissolved. Pour soup mixture into electric blender; add cream cheese, cover, and blend at high speed until smooth. Place onion, celery, pepper, mayonnaise, and shrimp in a bowl and toss to mix. Fold soup mixture into shrimp mixture. Mix well. Pour into 6-cup mold. Chill for several hours.

Sauce:

Dice 2 cucumbers and add 8 ounces sour cream and salt. Let sit over night.

–Mrs. Harold Bryson (Judy)

NOTE: I put this in a fish mold. Unmold on large silver tray covered with lettuce. Put an olive slice for the eye and pimento strips for gills. Arrange carrot curls, celery, and olives around fish. Shrimp mold can also serve as a cold meat dish or as a spread for party food.

TUNA BAKE WITH CHEESE SWIRLS (Serves 4)

3 T. chopped onions
⅓ c. chopped green pepper
3 T. butter or oleo
6 T. flour
1 t. salt
pepper
1 can chicken with rice soup
1½ c. milk
1 can tuna fish
1 T. lemon juice

Cook the onions and green pepper in the butter until soft; stir in flour, salt, pepper, and chicken soup. Add milk and cook until thick, stirring constantly. Add tuna and lemon juice. Pour into casserole and top with cheese swirls. Bake at 425° for 30 minutes. Serve piping hot.

Cheese Swirls:

Mix 1½-2 cups biscuit mix according to recipe. Roll biscuit dough ¼-inch thick; sprinkle thickly with grated cheese. Roll up as for jellyroll; slice roll, and lay on top of tuna casserole. Bake until done.

JOE'S LIP-SMACKING TUNA CASSEROLE (Serves 6-8)

1 (8 oz.) pkg. wide flat noodles
½ c. butter
5 T. flour
1 t. salt
¼ t. pepper
2½ c. milk
1 (8 oz.) pkg. cream cheese
1 (7 oz.) can drained tuna
½ lb. sliced mushrooms (fresh, if possible)
2 T. chives, chopped
1 (6 oz.) pkg. sliced Muenster cheese
1½ c. fresh bread crumbs

Cook noodles as package directs; drain and save. Melt 5 tablespoons of butter in a good-sized saucepan; stir in flour, salt, and pepper. Cook until bubbly, stirring constantly. Stir in milk slowly and heat until mixture thickens. Boil 1 minute. Slice cream cheese into sauce. Continue stirring until cheese is as melted as possible (small lumps are acceptable). Add tuna, mushrooms, and chives. Pour about ¾ cup of sauce into a greased 2½-quart casserole. Layer the ingredients on top as follows: half of the noodles, half of the remaining sauce, half of the Meunster cheese slices, half of the remaining sauce, rest of Meunster cheese slices, rest of sauce. Melt remaining 3 tablespoons of butter in small pan; stir in bread crumbs and mix with a fork. Sprinkle buttered crumbs over top of casserole. Bake in 350° oven for 30 minutes until crumbs brown a little.

–Joe Borgkvist, Jr.

SEAFOOD CASSEROLE (Serves 4-6)

1 c. bread (cubed)
1 c. cream (canned)
1 can crabmeat
1 can shrimp
6 hard-cooked eggs
1 c. mayonnaise (or less)
½ t. salt
½ t. pepper
chopped parsley
1 t. onion juice

Soften bread in cream. Mix all ingredients. Top with buttered crumbs. Bake in 350° oven. Cook until bubbly (35-45 minutes.)

–Mrs. Hugh Tobias (Marie)

Student Housing

Joy Rust

Vegetables

Cooking Rice

Vegetables and rice are a natural combination. Here are some hints for cooking a perfect batch of rice every time.

Standard procedure in cooking rice is to bring the designated amount of water to a rolling boil, add regular rice, cover immediately with a tight lid, and turn off the heat. Don't peek for 25 minutes. Drain and serve.

Never stir rice after it comes to a boil. It makes it gummy.

To keep rice from sticking, add 1 teaspoon oil to cooking water.

Add a few drops of Tabasco sauce to salted water to perk up the flavor of rice.

Add 2 teaspoons of vinegar to cooking water to give rice flavor.

Don't leave rice in the pot it was cooked in for more than 5-10 minutes or the rice will pack.

Rice can be refrigerated for about 1 week, if kept covered. It will freeze well for about 6-8 months. To reheat, place enough liquid in the bottom of a pan to keep the rice from scorching.

Cooking Vegetables

To retain vitamins and minerals when cooking vegetables, use as little water as possible. Avoid violent boiling of most vegetables.

Aromatic vegetables such as cabbage, carrots, and spinach will not develop an offensive odor—nor lose their food values—if cooked 12 minutes or less.

Do not throw away the water or juice from cooked vegetables. If you don't serve it with the vegetable, save it for soups or sauces or drink it plain.

Add sugar and a little lemon juice, not salt, to the cooking water for corn on the cob. Salt tends to toughen the kernels.

Season vegetables with ¼ stick butter, the juice of 1 lemon, and one of the following: (1) 1 teaspoon celery, poppy, and caraway seed; (2) ½ teaspoon garlic salt; (3) ¼ teaspoon powdered rosemary or marjoram. Try parsley as well.

Cauliflower is nothing more than a cabbage with a college education.

If you've always snapped beans, try slivering them or cutting them lengthwise.

To bake stuffed green peppers, use a greased muffin tin as a mold.

Onions: Peel and cut into quarters. Spread, one layer deep, on a pan and freeze. When frozen, quickly pack in bags or other freezer containers. Use as needed, chopping the still frozen onion on a board with a sharp, heavy knife.

Potatoes: First boil, then bake. If potatoes are boiled about 5 minutes, then put into a hot oven to bake, they will be thoroughly done in about half the usual time.

Potatoes soaked in saltwater for 20 minutes before baking will bake more rapidly.

Let raw potatoes stand in cold water for a few minutes before placing in skillet. This will lessen the tendency to shrink or curl.

ARTICHOKE CASSEROLE (Serves 6-8)

Layer in casserole, ending with cheese. If too dry, add a little water. Bake at 350° until hot through. *–Mrs. Genter Stephens (Dot)*

3 cans artichoke hearts, drained
½ c. olive oil
1 t. garlic purée
3 T. parsley flakes
salt and pepper to taste
2 c. flavored bread crumbs
½ c. Parmesan cheese

ASPARAGUS CASSEROLE I

Mix half of onion rings with all other ingredients. Top with remaining onion rings. Bake at 350° until bubbly.

–Mrs. Harold Alford (Kay)

1 can asparagus tips
2 hard-boiled eggs, diced
¾ c. grated cheese
1 can cream mushroom soup
½ can English peas
salt and pepper
1 can onion rings

ASPARAGUS SUPREME (Serves 4-6)

Pour asparagus tips into a 1-quart baking dish. Cover with mushroom soup. Top with onion rings. Bake in 350° oven until hot and bubbly, about 15 minutes.

–Mrs. Ray L. McKay (Marcia)

2 cans asparagus tips, drained
1 can cream of mushroom soup
1 (8 oz.) can fried onion rings

ASPARAGUS CASSEROLE II (Serves 4-6)

In a casserole dish, alternate layers of each of the above ingredients and top with cheese. Cover and bake at 350° for 45-60 minutes. Check after 30 minutes. Can also add chipped ham. *–Mrs. Claude Howe (Joyce)*

2 cans asparagus tips
4 hard-boiled eggs
1 can golden mushroom soup
cracker crumbs
grated cheese

BROCCOLI DELIGHT (Serves 4-6)

Mix all ingredients; put in buttered casserole dish. Bake in 350° oven for 30 minutes. *–Mrs. Dave Odom (Melissa)*

1 (10 oz.) pkg. chopped broccoli, thawed
1 small onion, minced
1 can cream mushroom soup
¼ c. slivered almonds
1 c. cooked rice
¼ c. oleo
1 (8 oz.) jar Cheese Whiz

BROCCOLI-RICE CASSEROLE (Serves 6)

Place the garlic cheese in the broccoli pan. Stir until melted. Add cooked rice, cream of mushroom soup. Add extra garlic salt, if desired. Place in greased casserole dish (may be made early and placed in refrigerator.) Bake at 350° until bubbly—about 45 minutes. Cover with grated cheese about 10 minutes before done.

–Mrs. Bill Rogers (Luwilda)

2 (10 oz.) pkg. cooked chopped broccoli, drained
1 roll garlic cheese, cut up
1 c. cooked rice
1 c. cream of mushroom soup
garlic salt (optional)

GREEN-BEAN CASSEROLE I (Serves 8)

Fry bacon till crisp, remove and set aside, sauté onion in bacon grease until tender. Stir in flour to make roux; cook over medium

6 strips bacon
½ c. chopped onion
2 T. flour
salt and pepper to taste

heat just to brown slightly, stirring constantly. Add juice from one can green beans, stir well until thickened. Add drained green beans, reserving liquid to be added if too thick. Mix well, adding cooked bacon, mustard, salt, and pepper. Melt margarine in small frying pan; add almonds and sauté 1 minute. Put almonds into green beans and heat thoroughly. If made ahead, place in 1½-quart casserole and heat in 350° oven about 30 minutes, or until bubbly. NOTE: Do not freeze.

Served at Pastors Conference, 1976

–The Committee

3 cans string beans, French-style
½ t. prepared mustard
1 T. margarine
¼ c. slivered almonds

GREEN BEAN CASSEROLE II (Serves 4-6)

Partially cook beans, remove from heat, drain, and stir in the butter. Mix other ingredients into the beans and pour all into a casserole dish. Bake uncovered at 350° for 20 minutes. Top with onion rings and bake 5-10 minutes longer.

–Miss Grace Johnson

2 (9 oz.) pkg. frozen French-style green beans, partially cooked
2 T. butter
½ envelope dry onion soup mix
½ cup sour cream
1 (10¾ oz.) cream of mushroom soup
1 (3 oz.) can French fried onion rings

DELUXE GREEN BEAN CASSEROLE (Serves 12)

Sauté onions and mushrooms in butter; add flour and brown. Add milk and cream; stir over low heat until smooth. Add cheese, seasonings, cooked beans, chestnuts. Pour into a large casserole dish and top with almonds. Bake 20 minutes at 350° or until bubbly. Can be frozen and cooked later.

–Mrs. David Sandifer (Jackie)

⅓ c. (1 stick) butter
1 chopped onion
8 oz. canned mushrooms
¼ c. flour
1⅔ c. milk
⅓ c. cream
½ lb. sharp cheese, grated (2½ c.)
1 t. salt
1 t. Accent
2 t. soy sauce
½ t. pepper
1 (5 oz.) can water chestnuts, sliced
2 pkg. frozen French-cut green beans (two 1-lb cans)
½ c. toasted slivered almonds

BEST GREEN BEANS (Serves 6)

Cut sausage in ¼-inch slices; cook slowly in heavy skillet. Add onions and pepper and cook 3-4 minutes. Add tomatoes and simmer 15 minutes. Add drained green beans and sprinkle a little salt. Heat well and serve.

–Mrs. Thomas Cobb (Lillie)

½ lb. stuffed sausage
3 T. chopped onion
1 T. chopped green pepper
1 (15 oz.) can tomatoes
1 (32 oz.) can whole green beans, drained

BEST BAKED BEANS (Serves 4-6)

Combine all but bacon in baking dish, stirring to mix. Arrange bacon or sausage on top. Bake 1 hour or until at desired degree of dryness. When pushed for time, start on top of stove in corningware dish until bubbly throughout, then put in oven.

–Mrs. Paul Frazer (Marilyn)

1 large can pork and beans
¼ c. chopped onions
¼ c. chopped bell pepper
¼ c. corn syrup
¼ c. brown syrup
1 T. prepared mustard
1-2 T. chili powder
1-2 T. Worcestershire sauce
Bacon strips or sliced smoked sausage

SAUCY BEANS AND RICE (Serves 6-8)

Heat sausage (sliced), beans, tomato sauce, water, salt, and pepper to taste. Cook 30 minutes (sliced green pepper is also good to add to this mixture). Pour over cooked rice.

–Mrs. Cecil Brasell (Candy)

1 pkg. (3 or 4) mild or hot long sausage
2 cans New Orleans-style red kidney beans
1 large jar thick and zesty tomato sauce
1½ c. hot water, rice

STOVETOP BEANS (Serves 2)

Mix ingredients in pan. Simmer about 10 minutes, stirring just enough to keep from sticking. (Too much stirring causes beans to crumble.) Serve while warm. NOTE: Recipe may also be used with pinto beans.

1 (16 oz.) can pork and beans
¼ c. catsup
dash minced onion
dash garlic powder (or minced garlic)
⅛ t. cinnamon
2 T. maple syrup

CABBAGE JAMBALAYA (Serves 4)

Sauté beef, onion, celery, and bell pepper. Season with salt and pepper, garlic salt, and Worcestershire sauce. Add tomatoes, chop-

1 lb. ground round
1 onion, chopped
1 stalk celery
1 bell pepper

ped cabbage, rice, and water. Cover and cook slowly until rice is done.

–Mrs. W. D. Stogner

salt and pepper to taste
dash garlic salt
dash Worcestershire sauce
1 can Rotel tomatoes
½ large head cabbage, chopped
¾ c. rice
1 c. water

CABBAGE FOR A KING (Serves 4)

Sauté onion in margarine until tender. Add flour and stir until smooth. Add tomatoes and seasonings. Cook cabbage in salted water for 5 minutes. Lightly brown the bread cubes in tablespoon of butter or margarine. Arrange the cabbage, tomato mixture, bread, and cheese in layers, ending with the bread and cheese. Bake in a moderate oven for 30 minutes.

–Mrs. Malcolm Tolbert (Nell)

½ c. chopped onion
3 T. margarine
3 T. flour
2 c. canned tomatoes
3 slices bread, cubed
2 t. Worcestershire sauce
¼ t. pepper
¼ lb. American cheese, shredded
¾ t. salt
½ t. sugar
6 c. finely shredded cabbage

FAR EAST CELERY (Serves 6-8)

Add celery to a small amount of salted boiling water. Cook gently 8 minutes or until tender. (Do not overcook.) Drain. Blend in the other ingredients. Place in a casserole. Sprinkle crackers over the top. Garnish with a slice of pimento. Bake at 350° for 35 minutes. *–Mrs. Bradford Curry (Catherine)*

4 c. celery, cut diagonally into ½-inch slices
¼ c. sliced almonds
1 can water chestnuts, thinly sliced
1 c. cream of chicken soup
6-8 Ritz crackers, crushed
¼ c. sliced pimento

CELERY WITH WATER CHESTNUTS (Serves 6)

Trim celery and slice into 1-inch pieces. Put into large saucepan. Add chicken broth, basil, salt, and pepper. Cover and cook until celery is tender but still crunchy (about 10 minutes). Blend cornstarch with water and gradually stir into hot stock; cook, stirring, just until thickened. Drain and slice water chestnuts; add to sauce along with almonds. Turn into 2-quart casserole. Mix bread crumbs with melted butter and sprinkle over top of vegetable. Bake, uncovered, in a 350° oven for 30 minutes.

–Mrs. David Sandifer (Jackie)

1 bunch celery
1 can regular-strength chicken broth
½ t. basil leaves
½ t. salt
¼ t. pepper
2 T. cornstarch
2 T. cold water
⅓ c. slivered almonds
1 (12 oz.) can water chestnuts
½ c. fine bread crumbs
3 T. melted margarine

CARROT-RING PLATTER

Fold in 4 beaten egg whites, stiff but not dry. Pour into well-buttered ring mold. Place in pan of water and bake at 350° for 40 minutes. To serve, turn upside down on damp serving platter.

Fill center of carrot ring with: 1 can small peas, without liquid, ½ can celery soup, undiluted, well heated in top of double boiler. Edge carrot ring with 2 (8 oz.) cans **tiny** whole beets, drained.

Make sauce:
1 c. milk
1 T. flour (heaping)
1 T. sugar
½ t. salt
½ stick butter

Add:
4 egg yolks
black pepper
1 small onion, grated

Add:
2 c. strained carrots (baby food ok)
1 c. cracker crumbs

Sauce:

Boil 5 minutes before adding beets. Cook slowly, stirring occasionally, until beets are heated. Add salt, pepper, and a tablespoon of butter. *–Mrs. H. Leo Eddleman (Sarah)*

¼ c. sugar
1 T. cornstarch
¼ c. beet juice
¼ c. vinegar

MARINATED CARROTS (Serves 8)

Cut round slices of carrots, onions, and pepper. Cook carrots long enough to be tender but not soft. Combine cooked carrot with onion and pepper. Using blender or mixer, beat the remaining ingredients and pour over cooked vegetable mix. Marinate overnight and serve cold. These carrots will be delicious as long as they last.

–Mrs. Ronnie Wright (Sarah)
Mrs. Jackie Hamilton (Barbara)
Mrs. Austin Dudley (Maurine)

2 lb. carrots
2 onions
1 large bell pepper
1 can tomato soup
½ c. salad oil
¾ c. vinegar
salt and pepper to taste
½ c. sugar
1 T. Worcestershire sauce
1 t. prepared mustard
2 onions

CORN PUDDING (Serves 6-8)

Combine corn, flour, sugar, and eggs. Add milk. Pour into well-greased 1½-quart oblong pan. Cut oleo on top. Cook in 350° oven for 45 minutes. TIP: If pudding is not firm (check by shaking), cook 15 minutes longer.

–Mrs. Harold Bryson (Judy)

1 pkg. frozen corn, thawed, or kernels of 6 fresh ears
2 T. flour
2 T. sugar
2 eggs
3 c. milk
½ stick oleo

SCALLOPED EGGPLANT (Serves 6)

Peel and dice eggplant. Cook in boiling salted water until tender (about 7 minutes). Drain. Mix eggplant, cream of mushroom soup, onion, and egg. Add ¼ cup stuffing; toss lightly. Pour into greased casserole. Finely crush ½ c. herbed stuffing and toss with butter. Sprinkle over top of casserole. Bake at 350° for 20 minutes.

–Mrs. Joe Nesom (Janice)

1 large eggplant, diced
½ t. salt
1 can cream of mushroom soup
1 egg, slightly beaten
½ c. chopped onion
¾ c. herb-seasoned stuffing
2 T. melted butter

EGGPLANT CREOLE (Serves 4-6)

Peel and dice eggplant; cook for 10 minutes in boiling salted water. Drain and place in greased baking dish. Melt butter; add flour; and stir until blended. Peel, slice, and chop onion. Add vegetables to the butter mixture with salt and bay leaf. Cook these ingredients for 5 minutes. Pour them over eggplant. Cover top with bread crumbs; dot lightly with butter or grated cheese. Bake in 350° oven for about 30 minutes.

–Miss Vivian Holder

1 medium eggplant
3 T. butter
3 T. flour
3 large fresh tomatoes or 2 c. canned tomatoes
1 small green pepper
1 small onion
1 t. salt
½ bay leaf
bread crumbs
grated cheese (optional)

EGGPLANT CASSEROLE (Serves 6)

Butter a 1½-quart casserole dish and sprinkle a layer of bread crumbs on the bottom. Add the squash or eggplant mixture; top with generous bits of butter, and cover with more bread crumbs. Bake at 350° for 30 minutes. NOTE: Can be frozen.

–The Committee

margarine
bread crumbs
2 c. cooled, mashed eggplant or squash
1 c. sour cream
1 grated carrot
pepper
1 can cream of mushroom soup
1 chopped onion
salt

SQUASH BALLS (Serves 8)

Mix all ingredients in order given; roll into balls and then in cornflake crumbs. Fry in

2 c. cooked squash
1 t. minced onion
1 egg

deep fat. Balls best when they have been refrigerated first.

–Mrs. Tim Williams (Glennis)

½ c. Bisquick
½ t. baking powder
salt and pepper to taste
cornflake crumbs

SQUASH CASSEROLE I (Serves 6)

Cook squash with onion; drain. Mash and salt and pepper to taste. Add all other ingredients except eggs. After mixture cooks slightly, add egg yolks. Let cool thoroughly. Fold in egg whites. Pour into greased 1½-quart casserole and bake at 300° for 45 minutes. *–Mrs. Jerry Barlow (Lynne)*

1 lb. yellow squash
1 medium onion
salt and pepper
1 c. grated Cheddar cheese
½ c. milk
1 T. butter
10 Saltine crackers, crushed
2 egg yolks
2 egg whites, beaten
salt and pepper to taste

SQUASH CASSEROLE II (Serves 6-8)

Cook squash (sliced) in hot water (salted) 8 minutes. Drain. Sauté onions and pepper in oleo. Add squash and mayonnaise; add cheese and chestnuts. Whip one egg and add sugar. Add to squash mixture. Place in 1½-quart casserole. Top with bread crumbs, and bake at 350° for 30 minutes.

–Mrs. Carl McLemore (Mary Elizabeth)

1½ lb. yellow squash (or 2 pkg. frozen)
½ c. oleo
½ c. chopped onions
¼ c. chopped bell peppers
½ c. mayonnaise
½ c. grated sharp cheese
1 c. sliced water chestnuts
1 egg
1 t. sugar
buttered bread crumbs

STUFFED POTATOES (Serves 4-5)

Bake potatoes. Mix other ingredients. Scrape the meat of the potato from the skin and mix with rest of ingredients. Salt and pepper to taste. Now re-stuff the shells. You might want to top with sliced cheese and return to the oven until the cheese is melted. If you do not have time to stuff the shells, just cube potatoes and boil. Then add the drained hot potatoes to the mixture and mix. Serve like mashed potatoes.

–Mrs. Chris Barbee (Brenda)

4 or 5 baking potatoes
½ c. chives
½ c. chopped green peppers
1 stick butter
1 (8 oz.) pkg. cream cheese
½ c. bacon bits (preferably all-vegetable type found in healthfood stores)

BAKED POTATOES AND BEEF (Serves 6)

Bake potatoes. When done, cut potatoes in half lengthwise; scoop out potatoes, saving shell. Brown meat, onion, and pepper in skillet. Drain fat. Add seasoning and catsup. Mash potatoes and combine with meat mixture. Fill shells with mixture. Sprinkle cheese on top. Bake in 400° oven for 15 minutes.

6 baking potatoes
1 lb. ground beef
¼ c. chopped onions
½ c. chopped pepper
2 t. salt
¼ t. nutmeg
½ t. pepper
½ c. catsup
1 c. cheese

POTATO SUPREME (Serves 4)

Mix well. Pour into buttered baking dish, either 9-by-13-inch or 2 smaller ones. Top with cornflakes. Dribble with melted oleo. Bake at 350° for 1 hour.

2 lb. frozen hashed brown potatoes, thawed
½ c. melted oleo
1 t. salt
½ t. pepper
1 can cream of chicken soup
½ c. finely chopped onion
1 pt. sour cream
10 oz. sharp or medium-sharp shredded cheese (or 1 can Cheddar cheese soup)

SWEET POTATO CASSEROLE (Serves 6)

To sweet potatoes add rest of ingredients in order given. Mix well. Pour into butter casserole and cover with the following: 1 c. light brown sugar, ⅓ c. plain flour, ⅓ c. melted oleo, 1 c. chopped pecans.

Mix and spread over potato mixture. Bake at 350° for about 35 minutes or until brown.

3 c. mashed sweet potatoes or 1 large can
2 eggs
⅓ c. evaporated milk
1 stick oleo
¾ c. sugar
1 t. vanilla
dash salt

SWEET POTATO ON PINEAPPLE (Serves 8)

Combine sweet potatoes, brown sugar, butter, orange juice, pumpkin pie spice, orange peel, pecans, and raisins. Drain pineapple slices and place in baking dish. Put ⅓ cup of sweet potato mixture on top of each pineapple slice. Bake at 375° for 20 minutes. Top each portion with a few marshmallows and bake 5 minutes longer.

–Mrs. Carl McLemore (Mary Elizabeth)

2 c. cooked, mashed sweet potato (1 large can)
⅔ c. brown sugar
¼ c. butter, melted
½ c. orange juice
1 t. pumpkin pie spice
1 t. grated orange peel
¼ c. chopped pecans
½ c. raisins
1 (20 oz.) can sliced pineapple
miniature marshmallows

SWEET POTATO BALLS (Serves 4)

Mix potatoes and brown sugar. Drop mixture onto wax paper containing crushed cornflakes. Before rolling into ball, place a marshmallow in the center. Roll in cornflakes and fry in deep fat to a golden brown.

–Mrs. Ray Davidson (Virginia)

4 medium-sized sweet potatoes, cooked and mashed
2 T. brown sugar, packed
crushed cornflakes
miniature marshmallows

MARSHMALLOW YAM BALLS (Serves 8)

Combine all ingredients except marshmallows and mash together well. Dip fingers in cold water and shape potato into a ball around 1 marshmallow. Roll or pat coconut on ball. Bake at 400° for 10 minutes.

–Mrs. Tim Dixon (Susan A.)

2 large cans sweet potato, drained
2 c. light brown sugar
2 lemons (grated peel and juice)
large marshmallows
coconut, flaked

SWEET POTATO SOUFFLÉ I (Serves 4-6)

Mix all ingredients well. Put in greased casserole dish.

3 c. sweet potato, mashed
2 eggs
½ c. oleo
1 c. sugar
1 t. vanilla

Topping:

Work together well. Sprinkle on top of potato mixture. Bake at 350° approximately 30 minutes. *–Mrs. James Blakney (Jan)*

⅓ c. oleo
⅓ c. flour
1 c. brown sugar
1 c. chopped nuts

SWEET POTATO SOUFFLÉ II (Serves 10-15)

Mix all ingredients together and pour into greased baking dish.

3 c. sweet potatoes, mashed (canned or fresh baked)
1 c. sugar
½ t. salt
2 eggs, lightly beaten
⅓ stick margarine, melted
½ c. sweet milk
1 t. vanilla

Topping:

Melt margarine; add sugar, flour, and nuts. Crumble over soufflé. Bake at 350° for 35 minutes.

–Mrs. Tommy Kinchen (Ruth Ann)

⅓ stick margarine
1 c. brown sugar
⅓ c. flour
1 c. chopped nuts

GLAZED LOUISIANA YAMS (Serves 4)

Drain syrup from yams and simmer until reduced by one-half. Add remaining ingredients and boil 2 minutes. Add yams and simmer until glazed and translucent. Add cherries to syrup during last 5 minutes of cooking and serve around yams for garnish.

–Mrs. Claude Howe (Joyce)

1 can yams
7 T. margarine
3 T. lemon juice
3 T. honey or 4½ T. brown sugar
1½ t. grated lemon rind
¾ c. cherries (fresh or canned)

PICKLED BLACK-EYED PEAS (Serves 4-6)

Mix all ingredients and allow to merinate at least 2 days before serving.

–Mrs. John McPherson (Marie)

1 (20 oz.) can black-eyed peas, drained
2 c. salad oil
1 clove garlic (or garlic powder)
½ t. salt
¼ c. wine vinegar
¼ c. onion, thinly sliced
black pepper

SEA BREEZE SPINACH MOLD (Serves 12-15)

In large bowl, dissolve unflavored gelatin in ¼ cup beef broth and ¼ cup cold water. (Don't use consomme, as it has a sweeter taste.) Heat to boiling remainder of beef broth and pour over dissolved gelatin, stirring until well dissolved. Fold in hard-boiled eggs, chopped spinach (thawed, drained, cooked, and chopped finer if there are large pieces), bacon or bacon bits, lemon juice, grated onion, mayonnaise, and salt and pepper to taste. Chill until firm.

–Mrs. Carl A. Hudson (Dottie)

2 envelopes unflavored gelatin
1 can beef broth
¼ c. cold water
4 hard-boiled eggs, chopped
1 box frozen chopped spinach
½ lb. bacon (or ½ jar bacon bits)
¼ t. lemon juice
1 small onion, grated
1 c. mayonnaise
salt and pepper to taste

SPINACH CASSEROLE (Serves 6)

Cook spinach according to directions. Add and mix other ingredients. Top with 1 cup seasoned dressing mix (not corn bread) that has been toasted in the margarine. Put in baking dish to cook. Bake at 350° for 30 minutes. *–Mrs. Jackie Hamilton (Barbara)*

3 pkg. frozen chopped spinach
1 pkg. onion soup mix
1 c. sour cream
1 c. seasoned dressing mix
½ c. oleo

SPINACH MADELEINE

Cook spinach as package directs, reserving ½ cup spinach water. Set spinach aside. Sauté onion in butter until tender. Add milk, water, flour, pepper, garlic salt, and cheese. Stir until cheese is melted. Add drained spinach. Put in casserole. Top with buttered bread crumbs and brown. NOTE: Can be made a day ahead and reheated in oven. *–Mrs. Landrum P. Leavell (Jo Ann)*

1 pkg. frozen chopped spinach
2 T. chopped onion
4 T. butter
½ c. evaporated milk
½ c. spinach water
2 T. flour
½ t. black pepper
¾ t. garlic salt
6 oz. roll Jalapeño cheese

VEGETABLE CASSEROLE (Serves 6)

Drain each vegetable but don't mix. Layer in casserole. Then mix other ingredients except onion rings and pour sauce over top. Bake in 350° oven for 20 minutes. Add onion rings.
Served at the Pastoral Division Christmas Dinner, 1976

1 can English peas
1 can lima beans
1 can green beans
1 c. mayonnaise
2 boiled eggs
½ medium onion, grated
1 T. Worcestershire sauce
dash Tabasco
1 T. prepared mustard
4 T. oil
1 can onion rings

CHINESE FRIED RICE (Serves 4)

Heat oil in large frying pan. Add meat and cook for about 1 minute, stirring constantly. Still stirring, add egg, salt, pepper and onions and cook until egg and meat are well mixed.

Add rice and soy sauce, and cook, stirring, until rice is thoroughly heated through. Turn out on platter, and garnish with chopped onions. *–Mrs. Grady Cothen (Bettye)*

2 T. oil or bacon drippings
2 c. chopped cooked shrimp, chicken, pork, or ham
1 egg, slightly beaten
½ t. pepper
¾ t. salt
2 green onions, chopped
4 c. cooked rice, cooled
2 T. soy sauce

RICE CASSEROLE I (Serves 4-6)

Sauté rice in melted margarine until brown, using medium heat. Combine mushrooms, chestnuts, soup, and salt in 2-quart casserole. Pour brown rice on top. Cover and bake at 350° for 1 hour.
–Mrs. Nelso Price (Trudy)

1 c. uncooked rice
2 T. margarine
1 (4 oz.) can mushrooms
1 (5 oz.) can water chestnuts
1 can onion soup, undiluted
½ t. salt

RICE CASSEROLE II (Serves 10)

1 c. raw rice
½ c. chopped onion
½ c. mushrooms, drained
¼ c. bell pepper, chopped
1 stick oleo
2 cans beef bouillon

Mix all ingredients in a 2-quart casserole dish. Cover and bake at 400° for 40 minutes. When doubled, use 3 cans bouillon.

–Mrs. Malcolm Tolbert (Nell)

CURRIED RICE (Serves 6-8)

2 T. chopped green onions
1 t. curry powder
4 T. butter or margarine
4 c. cooked rice
chipped parsley

In saucepan, cook onion with curry in butter until tender; toss with rice. Serve chicken over rice; garnish with parsley. Serve with a chicken casserole.

–Mrs. Mack P. Jones (Marie Martin)

Breads

When baking *corn bread*, if you like it brown, broil the cooked bread for about 30 seconds. Although good Southern cooks generally abhor sweet corn bread, there are some who will add a teaspoonful or two of sugar to the batter to promote browning.

For a *crustier corn bread*, first heat a greased skillet in the oven for 5 minutes, then pour in the batter. Always use a heavy metal utensil for making corn bread.

Try using *bacon grease* in place of oil for corn bread. It's wonderful for greasing pans, too.

If you like to brush a fresh loaf of bread with butter, do so *before* placing it in the oven rather than after. This will prevent a top crust's becoming speckled and wrinkled.

To prevent a crust from forming when *setting out dough to rise*, brush the top with water (not fat or butter) and keep it covered. If the crust is allowed to form, it will be worked through the bread when loaves are shaped and form little streaks throughout.

In order to prevent particles of fat being kneaded into the dough when *shaping into loaves*, place the dough to rise in an ungreased bowl. The fat causes breaks in the loaf and spots on the crust.

To test a dough for *sufficient rising*, press fingers gently into the dough. If indentations remain, the dough has risen enough. It will have doubled in bulk.

Add a teaspoon of ginger to *doughnuts* and they will not soak up fat.

To make *bread snails*, twist and hold one end of a ½-inch strip of basic yeast dough down on baking sheet. Wind strip around and around. Tuck end under.

To make *a figure eight*, hold one end of a ½-inch strip of yeast dough in one hand and twist the other end, stretching it until the two ends come together and make a figure eight.

To *frost rolls* or coffee cake, use the following recipe. Sift 1 cup

Patio Gates - Bunyun Building

Joy Rust

confectioner's sugar; moisten with 1 tablespoon of water, milk, or 1½ tablespoons of cream. Add ½ teaspoon of vanilla and spread.

Care of bread *after baking*: Upon taking bread from the oven, remove at once from pan and allow to cool uncovered in the fresh air. Do not brush the loaf with fat or sprinkle with water. When cold, the bread should be stored in a covered stone jar or in a tin breadbox. The jar or box should be washed, dried, and aired once a week.

When *freezing baked rolls and bread,* first cool bread to room temperature; second, wrap immediately with an airtight seal; third, freeze. Use aluminum foil to wrap and you can reheat in the same package.

When *reheating rolls or biscuits,* slip them into a paper bag, twist the top shut, and heat in a 400° oven for 8 minutes.

When baking *muffins*, remember not to overstir the batter; grease only the bottoms of the muffin cups (it gives muffins a better shape); and fill any batterless cups half full with water.

Before making *pancakes*, test the griddle by letting a few drops of water fall on it. If the water bounces and sputters ("dances" on the surface), the griddle is ready for cakes.

For a liquid equivalent to sour milk or buttermilk, place 1⅓ tablespoons vinegar (white vinegar makes a white product) in a standard measuring cup. Fill to the 1-cup mark with sweet milk or with diluted evaporated milk. Use 1½ tablespoons lemon juice for a similar result.

ANGEL BISCUITS

2 pkg. yeast
¼ c. lukewarm water
5 c. self-rising flour
1 t. soda
⅓ c. sugar
1 c. shortening
2 c. buttermilk

Dissolve yeast in water. Combine dry ingredients and work in shortening. Stir in yeast and buttermilk. Dough will seem too soft to handle. Handle gently on well-floured board with floured hands. Roll and shape as you like—biscuits or rolls. Bake in hot (400°) oven on middle rack. Unused dough may be kept in the refrigerator for as long as one week if kept well covered.

–Mrs. Bill Hinson (Bettye)

OLD-TIME BUTTERMILK BISCUITS (Makes 7-10 biscuits)

Sift flour into bowl. Add shortening and cut in with pastry blender. Add buttermilk; mix well; and turn out on lightly floured surface. Knead for 30 seconds; roll ½-inch thick. Place on well-greased baking pan; brush with melted shortening. Bake in hot (500°) oven for 8-10 minutes.

–Mrs. Eddie Kirkland (Alice)

2 c. sifted self-rising flour
2 T. vegetable shortening
1 c. buttermilk

SOUR CREAM BISCUITS

Sift dry ingredients together. Work in butter with tips of fingers or knife. Add sour cream and stir quickly and vigorously until it thickens. Press or roll to ½-¾-inch thickness. Brush tops with milk. Bake at 425° for about 12 minutes or until crust is browned evenly.

–Mrs. Ray Davidson (Virginia)

2 c. flour
½ t. salt
2½ t. baking powder
½ t. soda
2 T. butter
¾ c. thick sour cream

CHEESE BOXES

Melt butter and cheese over a slow fire. Beat egg whites until stiff. Add cheese mixture, beating until well blended. Use thin-sliced white bread (large loaf); take three slices at a time. Stack slices and cut off crusts. Cut stacks into quarters (4 boxes). Put slices in each box, together with cheese spread; use spread sparingly. Spread thinly like frosting around sides and top.

½ lb. butter
¾ lb. sharp cheese, cut fine
2 egg whites
1 giant loaf white bread, thin sliced

POPOVERS (Serves 12)

In mixer beat eggs, milk, flour, and salt. Add oil and beat 30 seconds. Fill 12 well-greased muffin tins half full. Bake at 475° for 10 minutes. Then bake at 350 for 15 minutes until brown. A few minutes before done, prick with fork to let steam escape.

–Mrs. Virginia Joyner

2 eggs
1 c. milk
1 c. flour
½ t. salt
1 T. oil

HOT DINNER ROLLS

Add melted shortening to cooled milk. Mix milk mixture with yeast mixture. Stir well. Add one slightly beaten egg. Add 1½ cup sifted flour. Cover and let rise about 1½ hours. Make in desired shapes or put in refrigerator until time to bake. Then let rise about 30 minutes before baking. Brush tops with melted butter. Bake at 375° for 25 minutes. *–Mrs. Charles Woody (Cheryl)*

Mix together:
1 pkg. dry yeast
1 c. flour
¼ c. sugar
1 t. salt

Melt:
¼ c. shortening
1 c. milk, scalded then cooled

MAYONNAISE QUICK BREAD (Makes 9 rolls)

Mix all ingredients. Drop dough into a greased (or Teflon) muffin pan and bake at 350° for 10-15 minutes. NOTE: If mixture is too thick, add a little more milk.

–Mrs. Robert Neese (Beth)

1 c. self-rising flour
1 T. mayonnaise
¼ c. milk

QUICKIE YEAST ROLLS (Makes 12-18 rolls)

Mix first four ingredients then add self-rising flour. Stir. Roll and shape dough or cut out with round cookie cutters. Let rise 45-60 minutes. Bake at 425° for 10 minutes. Melt butter on top after cooking.

–Mrs. Bill Davis (Linda)

¾ c. warm water
1 pkg. dry yeast
¼ c. sugar
¼ c. oil
2 c. self-rising flour

HURRY-UP ROLLS (Makes 50 rolls)

Put ½ cup milk in bowl. Add sugar, salt, and butter. When lukewarm to touch, dissolve yeast cakes in the other half of the milk. Add to first mixture. Add flour and stir well. Let rise 15 minutes. Put on a floured board. Shape into rolls. Place in buttered pan. Let rise no more than 30 minutes. Bake in 400° oven for 15 minutes. Total time to mix, rise, and bake is 1 hour.

–Mrs. Gary Arflin (Robin W.)

1 c. milk, scalded
1½ T. sugar
1½ t. salt
1 T. butter
2 yeast cakes
2½ c. flour

HOMEMADE WHITE BREAD (Makes 28 slices)

Dissolve yeast in water. Mix egg, sugar, salt, and add to yeast mixture. Stir in melted oleo and add flour a little at a time, stirring well after each addition. Cover and let rise until doubled in bulk. Punch down, knead, and put into 2 greased loaf pans. Let rise, then bake at 350° until done and brown on top.

–Mrs. James Richardson

1 pkg. dry yeast
2 c. lukewarm water
1 egg, beaten
½ c. sugar
5 T. oleo, melted
5 c. flour (enough for stiff dough)
pinch salt

REFRIGERATOR WHEAT BREAD (Makes 2 loaves)

Mix 2½ cups all-purpose flour with yeast. Heat milk, water, ¼ cup oil, sugar, and salt over low heat until warm (120-130°). Add liquid ingredients to flour yeast mixture and beat 3 minutes on high speed of electric mixer. Add whole wheat flour; gradually stir in more white flour to make a stiff dough. Turn out onto lightly floured surface and knead 5-10 minutes. Cover dough with bowl or pan and let rest 20 minutes. Divide in half. Roll each half out to 7-by-14-inch rectangle. Roll with narrow side, pressing dough into roll at each turn. Press ends to seal and fold under loaf. Place in two greased 4½-by-8½-inch loaf pans. Brush loaves with oil. Cover with plastic wrap. Refrigerate 2-24 hours. When ready to use, let stand at room temperature 10 minutes. Puncture any gas bubbles with skewer. Bake in preheated 400° oven for 40 minutes. Makes two 1-pound loaves.

–Mrs. Thomas Cobb (Lillie)

3½-4 c. all-purpose flour
2 pkg. dry yeast
2 c. milk
¾ c. water
¼ c. oil
3 T. sugar
1 T. salt
4 c. whole wheat flour

WHOLE WHEAT ROLLS OR BREAD

Soften yeast in water to which has been added the 1 teaspoon of sugar. Scald milk and pour over the ½ cup of sugar and the shortening. Allow to cool and add beaten eggs. Mix in yeast. Add sifted flour and salt. Allow to rise once to double its size, then

3 yeast cakes
¼ c. lukewarm water
1 t. sugar
2 c. milk
½ c. sugar (may use honey)
2 T. shortening
2 eggs

shape into roll or loaves and bake in 400° oven for approximately 20 minutes. A nutritious and sweet brown bread.

–Mrs. Fisher Humphreys (Caroline)

5 c. whole wheat flour
2 t. salt

REFRIGERATOR BRAN ROLLS

Combine butter, sugar, salt, and bran in large bowl. Add boiling water; let stand until lukewarm. Dissolve yeast in ½ cup warm water. Add yeast and beaten eggs to other water. Add half of flour and beat until smooth. Add remaining flour; mix. Cover and store in refrigerator until ready to use. Punch down dough. With floured hands, shape ball of dough to fill oiled muffin cups about half full. Let rise in a warm place 2-2½ hours. Bake in preheated 425° oven for 12-15 minutes. Can store several days.

–Mrs. Jerry Garrard (Ruthie)

1 c. butter
½ c. brown sugar
2 t. salt
2 c. 100% bran (found in health food stores)
1¾ c. boiling water
2 T. dry yeast
½ c. warm water
2 eggs
6 c. whole wheat or unbleached flour

REFRIGERATOR ROLLS

Combine first four ingredients in large mixing bowl and stir until shortening is dissolved. Sprinkle yeast in water and let it set until first mixture is just lukewarm. Stir the yeast mixture into the first mixture and mix well. Beat egg and add it to mixture, stirring well. Sift flour and gradually add, stirring alternately. Cover and store in refrigerator until ready to use. Punch down dough. Shape to fit muffin pans. Let rise till doubled. Bake at 425° for 12-15 minutes.

–Mrs. Gary Hadden (Marilyn)

1 c. hot water
6 T. shortening
1 t. salt (rounded)
¼ c. granulated sugar
1 pkg. yeast
2 T. lukewarm water
1 egg
3½-4 c. plain flour

YUMMY NO-CRUMBLE CORNBREAD

Combine first 4 ingredients in mixing bowl, stirring well with fork. Heat margarine and shortening in 10-inch cast iron skillet over medium flame until melted.

To dry ingredients, add milk and beaten

1½ c. yellow corn meal
¾ c. whole wheat flour (white can be used but might crumble)
1½ t. salt
1½ t. baking powder

egg. Mix well. Then add melted butter and shortening (be sure to leave a little in the skillet). Mix well again. Pour into hot skillet, and place over medium flame for 5 minutes (this makes a good bottom crust). Then bake in 475° oven for 12-15 minutes.

–Mrs. Danny Chapman (Margaret)

3 T. margarine
¼ c. shortening
1 c. milk
1 egg, beaten

MEXICAN CORNBREAD

Mix eggs, sour cream, oil, and corn together. Add the chopped onion and chopped chile peppers. Sift dry ingredients and add to mixture. Grease and heat one big iron skillet in 350° oven. Pour in half the mixture, add the cup of cheese evenly, and cover all with the remaining batter. Cook in 350° oven for approximately 30-35 minutes or until golden brown. *–Mrs. Genter Stephens (Darothy)*

2 eggs
1 c. sour cream
2 T. oil
1 can cream-style corn
1 onion, chopped
1 can green chiles, chopped
1 c. self-rising cornmeal
1 t. salt
2 t. baking powder
½ t. baking soda
1 c. grated cheese

SOUR CREAM CORN BREAD (Serves 4)

Mix all ingredients together. Pour into greased 9-by-9-by-2-inch pan. Bake at 400° for 30 minutes. Freezes well if you have any left over. Just wrap in foil and reheat.

–Mrs. John F. Gibson

1 c. self-rising corn meal
¼ c. oil
2 eggs
1 c. sour cream
1 c. cream-style corn

OLD-TIME CORN BREAD (Serves 6)

Preheat oven to 450°. Into mixing bowl, sift dry ingredients; add the egg, oil, and buttermilk; and mix well. Fill well-greased and floured iron skillet or muffin pans to two-thirds full. Bake.

–Mrs. Eddie Kirkland (Alice)

1½ c. self-rising corn meal
½ c. sifted flour
1 egg
3 T. melted butter or oil
1¼ c. buttermilk

HUSH PUPPIES I

Sift corn meal, flour, baking powder, salt, and baking soda together. Stir in onion and

⅓ c. stone ground corn meal
⅓ c. sifted unbleached flour
1 t. baking powder

pepper. Add egg and milk. Drop batter by teaspoonfuls into hot grease. Drain

–Mrs. Jerry Garrard (Ruthie)

1 t. salt
1 t. baking soda
¼ c. chopped onion
¼ c. chopped green peppers
1 egg, beaten
1 c. buttermilk

HUSHPUPPIES II (Serves 6)

1½ c. self-rising corn meal
1 T. sugar
1 c. chopped onions
2 eggs

Mix in enough milk to moisten so they'll stick together. Mix and drop by spoonfuls into hot grease. Cook until brown.

–Mrs. Mack P. Jones (Marie Martin)

DILLY BREAD (Serves 6)

1 unbeaten egg
1 pkg. active dry yeast or 1 cake compressed yeast
¼ c. warm water
1 c. creamed cottage cheese
2 T. sugar
1 T. minced onion or onion soup mix
1 T. butter
2 t. dill seed
¼ t. soda
1 t. salt
2¼-2½ c. flour

Dissolve yeast in warm water. Combine: cottage cheese, sugar, onion, butter, dill seed, salt, soda, egg, and yeast. Add flour a portion at a time to form a stiff dough, beating well after each addition. (For first addition of flour, use mixer on medium speed.) Cover and let rise in warm place until light and doubled in size, about 50-60 minutes. Stir down dough. Turn into well-greased 8-inch round 1-2-quart casserole. Let rise in warm place until light, 30-40 minutes. Bake at 350° for 40-50 minutes until golden brown. Brush with soft butter and sprinkle with salt. You can bake this bread early in the day and still serve it warm at dinner time by wrapping it in aluminum foil and placing it in a 350° oven for about 15 minutes.

–Mrs. Harold Bryson (Judy)

BRAN MUFFINS BY THE PAILFUL (Serves 10)

Set aside to cool:
2 c. boiling water
2 c. seedless raisins
5 t. soda

Cream together:
1 c. shortening or oleo
2 c. sugar

Add the dry ingredients to the wet mixture, alternating with the cooled water and raisins prepared at the beginning. Store in a tight container and wait until the next day to bake the first muffins. This will keep in the refrigerator from 4-6 weeks. Bake at 350° about 20-25 minutes.

–Mrs. Maurine Dudley Austin

Add to the creamed mixture:
4 eggs
1 qt. buttermilk

Mix together:
5½ c. sifted flour
4 c. bran buds
2 c. 40% branflakes
1 t. salt

RAISIN BRAN MUFFINS

Mix dry ingredients in very large bowl. Add liquids and mix. Bake at 400° for 15-20 minutes. Store in covered container in refrigerator. Will keep up to 6 weeks in refrigerator. *–Mrs. Paul Robertson (Judy)*

1 (5 oz.) box raisin bran cereal
5 c. flour
2 t. salt
3 c. sugar
5 t. baking soda
1 c. cooking oil
1 qt. buttermilk
2 T. vanilla
6 eggs, beaten
1 T. apple or pumpkin pie spice

OATMEAL MUFFINS (Makes 12 muffins)

Preheat oven to 400°. Grease only bottoms of muffin cups. In medium bowl, with fork, stir milk, egg, and salad oil until well mixed. Add remaining ingredients and stir just until flour is moistened. Batter will be lumpy. Spoon batter into cups, filling each two-thirds full. Bake 20-25 minutes until golden brown and toothpick inserted in center comes out clean. *–Dr. Helen E. Falls*

1 c. milk
1 egg
2 T. salad oil
1 c. flour
¾ c. quick-cooking oats
¼ c. sugar
1 t. baking powder
1 t. salt

GOUGÈRE (Serves 6)

Preheat oven to 375°. Put milk in a saucepan with butter and heat over low heat. When butter is melted, add salt and dump in flour all at once. Stir well over heat until mixture leaves sides of pan. Add 1 egg at a time, beating very hard. (Move pan off heat). Mixture will be very thick. Add cream and ½ cup cheese. Mix well and form a mound in a well greased 10-inch glass pie pan. Sprinkle top with shredded cheese. Bake 25 minutes and

1 c. milk
⅓ c. butter
¼ t. salt
1 c. sifted flour
4 large eggs
1 T. heavy cream
½ c. shredded Swiss or Gruyère
3 T. shredded cheese

then turn oven to 350° for 10 minutes more. Serve hot with butter.

–Mrs. Dave R. Odom (Melissa)

ONION-CHEESE BREAD (Serves 4)

Cook onion in shortening until tender and light brown. Combine egg and milk, add to Bisquick mix, and stir until dry ingredients are just moistened. Add onion and half of cheese. Spread dough in greased 8-by-1½-inch round baking dish. Sprinkle top with remaining cheese and poppy seeds; drizzle melted butter over all. Bake in hot (400°) oven 20-25 minutes. Serve hot.

–Dr. Helen E. Falls

½ c. chopped onion
1 T. shortening
1 beaten egg
½ c. milk
1½ c. Bisquick
1 c. grated sharp American cheese
1 T. poppy seeds
2 T. melted butter or margarine

SWEET ROLLS

Combine above mixtures and add 1 egg, beaten, and 3½ cups flour. Let rise until double in size. Divide dough in half and roll into large rectangle. Brush with melted butter. Sprinkle with brown sugar/cinnamon mixture. Roll up jellyroll fashion. Cut in 1-inch pieces. Place in greased muffin pans. Do same with other half of dough. Let rise until doubled. Bake at 250° until brown. Cover with powdered sugar/milk frosting.

–Mrs. Bill Rogers (Luwilda)

Stir the following in a small bowl until dissolved:
6 T. vegetable shortening
1 t. salt
½ c. sugar
1 c. hot water

Let the following dissolve in a large bowl:
1 pkg. yeast
¼ c. lukewarm water
¼ c. sugar

APRICOT SNACK LOAF

Preheat oven to 375°. In mixing bowl, cover dried apricots with warm water and let stand 15 minutes. Drain and cut into pieces. In another bowl combine flour, sugar, baking powder, salt, and soda. Add shortening, egg, orange juice, and water. Mix well. Stir in apricots and nuts. Grease bottom of 9-by-5-inch pan and bake 45-55 minutes. Remove from pan. *–Dr. Helen E. Falls*

1 c. dried apricots
2 c. flour
1 c. sugar
2 t. baking powder
1 t. salt
¼ t. soda
¼ c. shortening
1 egg
½ c. orange juice
¼ c. water
½ c. chopped nuts

ZUCCHINI BREAD (Serves 6)

Beat together first three ingredients. Then add 2 cups peeled and grated raw zucchini. Sift together the remaining ingredients and add to first mixture.

3 eggs
1½ c. sugar
1 c. vegetable oil
3 c. flour
1 t. soda
¼ t. baking powder
1 t. salt
3 t. cinnamon
1 t. allspice
1 t. cloves
½ t. nutmeg
1 t. vanilla

CANADIAN CHERRY NUT BREAD (Serves 8)

Drain cherries and cut in small pieces. Mix sugar and egg and sift baking powder, salt, and flour. Add alternately with milk. Add cherries and nuts, then the butter. Pour into well-greased loaf pan and bake at 350° for 45 minutes. Serve warm or freeze. When serving, slice, butter, and broil a minute or two. Best with hot tea as it is served in Canada.

–Mrs. George Harrison (Jean)

1 bottle maraschino cherries
1 c. brown sugar
1 egg
2 t. baking powder
½ t. salt
2 c. flour
1 c. cherry juice and milk (combined)
¾ c. nuts (preferably walnuts)
1 T. butter

SANDWICH LOAF (Serves 8)

Slice bread horizontally into 4 layers. Stack alternately white bread and whole wheat with egg salad, ham salad, and chicken salad. Finished loaf would have: 1 layer white bread / 1 layer egg salad / 1 layer whole wheat bread / 1 layer ham salad / 1 layer white bread / 1 layer chicken salad. TIP: *Homemade* bread makes a better loaf. Makes 2 loaves. Cover entire outside of loaves with cream cheese that has been beaten with milk. Ice loaves like a cake and sprinkle with fresh parsley. Keep in refrigerator and cover with a wet towel.

–Mrs. Bill Rogers (Luwilda)

1 loaf unsliced white bread
1 recipe chicken salad
1 recipe egg salad
1 loaf unsliced whole wheat bread
1 recipe ham salad

KONA INN BANANA BREAD (Serves 16)

Cream shortening and sugar until light; add eggs; beat well. Stir in banana; add sifted dry ingredients to banana mixture. Pour into greased 9-by-9-by-2-inch pan. Bake for 30-35 minutes in moderate (350°) oven.

–Mrs. Weldon Fortenberry (Georgia)

Mrs. Fortenberry writes: "Kona is the second largest city on the 'Big Island,' Hawaii. The Kona Inn is known for this cakelike banana bread."

½ c. shortening
1 c. sugar
2 eggs
¾ c. mashed ripe bananas
1¼ c. sifted cake flour
¾ t. soda
½ t. salt

Carey Hall

Desserts

Cakes

Eggs fresh from the barnyard (not yet put in cold storage) make the most *delicate cakes*, but to be beaten successfully, they need to be about four days old. Since it is impossible to beat as much air into eggs that have been preserved in cold storage, it is better to use fresh eggs, especially for the true sponge cakes and angel food. These cakes depend upon the air that is beaten into eggs for leavening.

Egg yolks can't hold as much air as egg whites because the yolks contain a large amount of fat. Poorly beaten egg yolks can result in a *heavy* or *soggy cake* or can cause a compact streak to form at the bottom.

Egg whites help to make a cake light. That's because a lot of air can be trapped in them by beating. For best results, remove eggs from refrigerator before using; allow them to reach a cool room temperature (65-70°). Eggs beat up lighter and more quickly when not too cold. This is of special importance in making angel food cake. Underbeaten or overbeaten egg whites make cake of poor volume.

To *save on sugar,* substitute corn syrup or honey or use recipes sweetened with molasses or other syrup. A recipe that calls for a few tablespoons of sugar is usually successful if made with the same amount of corn syrup or honey. However, since honey is sweeter than sugar, corn syrup only about half as sweet, and both honey and corn syrup contain water, more care must be taken in making larger substitutions.

For best results in *creaming shortening*, let stand at room temperature before using. It should be "plastic"—just soft enough to be worked readily with a spoon. Do not allow shortening to become soft, and do not melt it even slightly. If too soft, shortening will not cream properly and may cause a coarse grain and poor volume in cake.

Raisins heated a moment in the oven will not sink to the bottom of the cake.

Three teaspoons vanilla and 1 teaspoon almond extract may be used to substitute for *pistachio flavoring.*

A cake is done when it springs back when lightly touched in the center. It will also pull away slightly from the edge of the pan.

The layers of a cake will come out of their pans without sticking if you will set the hot pans on a damp cloth when they come out of the oven.

Pans for *butterless cakes*, such as sponge and angel food, should never be oiled, floured, or lined with paper.

To split cake layer, insert wooden picks at the halfway mark all around the layer. Ride blade of serrated knife on picks, cutting in toward the center all around. Cut right across and through.

Jellyrolls are neater to roll if you use the towel trick. When the roll is filled and ready, start first tight turn with your hand; then lift towel higher and jellyroll will roll by itself.

When your *cooked icing* is ready to spread on a cake, add a small amount of butter to warm icing and allow to melt. This will keep the icing from hardening and flaking off, no matter how old it gets.

To frost *cupcakes* quickly, dip the tops of cooled cupcakes into a bowl of fluffy frosting. Give your wrist a slight twist and quickly pull cupcake out. Frosting should be soft for this.

Cookies

When making *rich butter cookies,* mix the dry ingredients thoroughly with the creamed mixture. Otherwise, the dough will be crumbly.

For a quick trick in *shaping your favorite drop cookies,* just fill a pastry bag with dough, but don't use a metal tip. Press out just the right amount of dough onto the cookie sheet and flatten.

Flat *baking sheets* or those with very low sides will let your cookies bake evenly and quickly. For best circulation of heat and thus for even baking, non-Teflon baking sheets should be shiny. All sheets should be narrow enough to clear the sides of the oven by at least 2 inches.

Cool baking sheets before placing cookie dough on them or the heat will melt the shortening in the dough, causing cookies to spread too much during baking.

Keep *soft cookies* soft by placing a slice of bread in their storage container.

If *crisp cookies* soften in storage, place them in a 300° oven for about 5 minutes.

Pies

When *rolling pastry,* lightly flour your surface and rolling pin, taking only enough dough for a single crust; roll pastry from the center to the edges, rolling until thin, less than ⅛-inch thick.

Roll the circle of your pastry so that it will be large enough to extend 1½-inches all around the edge of an inverted pie pan. The pastry may be transferred to the pan either by rolling it around the rolling pin or by folding it into quarters.

To seal the edges of a *double-crust pie*, moisten the bottom edge and press top and bottom edges together, then fold the edge of the top crust under the bottom crust and press together firmly. Flute. Allow the steam that forms when baking a double-crust pie to escape by cutting slits in the top crust. If you have an artistic bent, make a pretty pattern with the slits.

When you want a shiny, attractive *glaze on a pie,* brush the top crust with egg white beaten with a little water or cream.

If the fluted edge of your *crust browns too quickly,* cover it with aluminum foil for the remaining baking time.

Juicy *fruit pies* frequently boil over; a sheet of aluminum foil strategically placed on the rack below to catch drips saves a lot of postbaking cleanup time.

To avoid a skin on the top of *cooked pudding and pie fillings,* and to keep the pudding nice and creamy, press plastic wrap directly on top of hot filling. Cool, then refrigerate. Peel plastic when pudding is set and you are ready to serve.

EASY CREPES (Makes 18)

¾ c. all-purpose flour
1 T. sugar
½ t. salt
cinnamon (optional)
1 c. milk
2 eggs
2 T. oil

Put flour, sugar, and salt into a bowl. Make a well in the center and pour in milk and eggs. Stir and beat until perfectly smooth. Batter should be as thin as coffee cream. If necessary, add a little extra milk. Heat a 5-inch frying pan (or follow directions for a crepe pan). Pour in a few drops of salad oil and tip so that the bottom of the pan glistens with a thin film of oil. Pour in 2 or 3 tablespoons of batter, just enough to thinly cover the pan. Tilt so that mixture spreads evenly. Cook on one side. Turn and cook on the other side. Crepes can be filled with just about anything for dinner or dessert. TIP: A small 4- or 5-inch iron skillet is excellent for mak-

ing crepes. They freeze well. Stack with a layer of waxed paper between each crepe.
–Mrs. Harold Bryson (Judy)

CREPE FILLING WITH STRAWBERRY SAUCE (Serves 18)

Filling:

Place cream cheese in small bowl; let stand until room temperature and soft. Beat in sugar, lemon rind, and juice until mixture is smooth and fluffy. Spoon about 2 tablespoons filling across each crepe and roll up, placing the fold side down in shallow ovenproof pan.

Filling:
12 oz. cream cheese
¼ c. sugar
1½ t. grated lemon rind
3 T. lemon juice

Topping:

Stir all ingredients together in double boiler. Stir occasionally over a warming temperature. Leave it on to simmer, and cover until serving time. If you prepare rolled crepes on the morning of the dinner, cover with plastic wrap so they won't dry out.

Topping:
1 (12 oz.) pkg. frozen sliced strawberries
1 T. lemon juice
¼ t. almond extract
¼ c. slivered, blanched almonds

To serve:

Heat filled crepes in 400° oven for 10 minutes or until piping hot. Spoon hot sauce on top. *–Mrs. Harold Bryson (Judy)*

CHEESE CAKE (Serves 8-10)

Beat eggs until thick; add sugar. Beat well. Add cheese and vanilla. Will take about 10 minutes of beating with mixer on high speed. Pour into crust and put in preheated 350° oven. Bake 35 minutes; remove and add topping.

Crust:
1 pkg. zwieback, rolled
2 T. sugar
1 t. cinnamon
¼ c. melted oleo

Mix and press into pan:
4 eggs
1 t. vanilla
1½ c. sugar
3 (8 oz.) pkg. cream cheese

Topping:

Return to oven and bake 10 minutes longer.
–Mrs. Landrum P. Leavell (Jo Ann)

1 carton (1 c.) sour cream
1 t. vanilla
1 c. sugar

PEACHES 'N CREAM CHEESECAKE (Serves 8-10)

¾ c. flour
½ t. salt
3 T. butter or margarine
1 egg
1 t. baking powder
1 (3¼ oz.) pkg. dry vanilla pudding mix (not instant)
½ c. milk

Combine all ingredients in large mixer bowl. Beat two minutes at medium speed. Pour into greased bottom and sides of 9-inch-deep dish. Add 1 (15-20 oz.) can of sliced peaches or pineapple chunks, well drained; reserve juice. Place over batter. Combine 1 (8 oz.) package of softened cream cheese, ½ cup sugar, and 3 tablespoons reserved juice in a small mixer bowl, and beat 2 minutes at medium speed. Spoon to within 1 inch of the batter. Combine 1 tablespoon sugar, ½ teaspoon cinnamon, and sprinkle over cream cheese filling. Bake at 350° for 30-35 minutes until crust is golden brown. Filling will appear soft. Store in refrigerator. Serves 8-10.

–Mrs. Jim Gallery (Debra)

CHEESE CAKE (Serves 10)

1 (8 oz.) pkg. cream cheese
1 pkg. lemon jello
15 double graham cracker
¾ c. sugar
1 c. boiling water
1 large can evaporated milk, chilled
1 stick butter

Make pie shell of cracker crumbs and melted butter in 9-by-12-inch pyrex dish. Dissolve jello in hot water. Set aside to cool. Mix cream cheese (at room temperature) and sugar thoroughly. Whip chilled milk until stiff. Add cheese mix to jello and stir in whipped milk. Pour into prepared shell (hold back ¼ graham cracker mixture) and sprinkle on top. Refrigerate or freeze indefinitely. May be served plain or with fruit topping.

–Mrs. James Taylor (Maidee)

BLUEBERRY TORTE (Serves 8)

1 can blueberry pie filling
1 stick oleo
½ box white cake mix
½ to 1 c. pecans

Spread pie filling in oblong dish and cover with cake mix. Slice oleo over this and sprinkle with pecans. Cook at 325° for about 35-40 minutes. (Cherry or strawberry pie filling can be used.) To make large torte use 2 cans pie filling and 1 box of cake mix.

BLUEBERRY CREAM FLUFF (Serves 8-10)

Melt marshmallows in milk in top of double boiler. Cool. Fold in whipped cream and blueberry filling. Pour into crust and chill. Other fruit fillings can be used. This is delicious! *–Mrs. Dave R. Odom (Melissa)*

½ c. milk
½ pint heavy cream (whipped, or 1 container Cool Whip)
1 (10 oz.) pkg. tiny marshmallows
1 can blueberry pie filling
1 graham cracker crust

HORATIO'S BURNT CREME (Serves 6)

Preheat oven to 350°. Heat cream over low heat until bubbles form around edge of pan. Beat egg yolks and sugar together until thick, about 3 minutes. Gradually beat cream into egg yolks. Stir in vanilla and pour into 6 (6 ounce) custard cups. Place custard cups in baking pan that has about ½ inch water in the bottom. Bake until set, about 45 minutes. Remove custard cups from water and refrigerate until chilled. Sprinkle each custard with about 2 teaspoons granulated sugar. Place on top rack under broiler and cook until topping is medium brown. Chill before serving.

–Mrs. Weldon Fortenberry

Mrs. Fortenberry writes: "Horatio's is a famous restaurant in Honolulu, on the island of Oahu. This is their dessert specialty."

1 pt. whipping cream
4 egg yolks
½ c. granulated sugar
1 T. vanilla extract
granulated sugar for topping

CHOCOLATE ICEBOX DESSERT (Serves 6-8)

This dessert must be prepared 1 day ahead of serving. Use a spring mold pan, not greased. Crumble macaroons in the bottom. Make a crown of lady finger halves. Cream butter and powdered sugar. Add chocolate (melted) and 4 egg yolks, one at a time. Beat 4 egg whites and fold into mixture. Add vanilla and almond extracts. Put in pan. Let it set a day in the refrigerator. Add whipped cream just before releasing from the mold.

–Mrs. Bill Rogers

1 doz. almond macaroons
1 pkg. lady fingers
3 sticks butter
1 box powdered sugar
4 sq. semi-sweet chocolate
4 eggs; separated
1 t. vanilla
1 t. almond extract
1 pt. whipped cream

PEACH CUSTARD TRIFLE (Serves 12-15)

Into a 1-quart saucepan turn the dessert mix; gradually stir in 1 cup of the milk. Over low heat, stirring constantly to prevent sticking, bring to a full boil. Remove from heat; stir in ¼ teaspoon of the almond extract. Pour into a bowl; chill until firm. Drain peaches, reserving ½ cup of their syrup. Line bottom and sides of a serving dish (about 11-by-7½-inches). Sprinkle cake with reserved peach syrup mixed with remaining ¼ teaspoon almond extract. Arrange peaches over cake. Refrigerate. To chilled dessert mix add whipped topping mix and remaining ¾-cup milk; beat until light and fluffy and mixture holds soft peak; spread over peaches. Refrigerate until ready to serve. Garnish with whipped cream, cherries, and almonds. *–The Committee*

1 (2½ oz.) pkg. custard flavor dessert mix
½ t. almond extract
1 frozen pound cake, thawed and cut into ½-inch slices
1 (2 oz.) pkg. whipped topping mix
1 ¾ c. milk
1 (29 oz.) can sliced peaches, drained
½ c. heavy cream, whipped
maraschino cherries

DESSERT DUMPLINGS

First make sauce. Then make dumplings. To mix, sift flour; measure and sift with baking powder, sugar, and salt. Cut in ¼ cup butter; add milk and vanilla. Mix quickly and drop by teaspoonfuls into boiling caramel sauce. Cover and cook gently for 20 minutes. *Do not lift cover.* Top with whipped cream or vanilla ice cream. *–Mrs. Dennis Rogers (Judy)*

Dumplings:
1½ c. flour
⅓ c. sugar
¼ c. butter
½ t. vanilla
1½ t. baking powder
¼ t. salt
⅔ c. milk

Sauce:
2 T. butter
¼ t. salt
1½ c. brown sugar
1½ c. boiling water

RITZ TORTE

Roll crackers well. Add baking powder, vanilla, and pecans. Add sugar to beaten egg whites and beat well. Fold into cracker mixture and bake 30 minutes at 350° in a greased 9-inch pan. Let cool and top with cream. Chill at least 3 hours. Decorate with shaved German chocolate if desired.

–Mrs. Julian Stephens, Jr. (Tamara)

20 Ritz crackers
3 egg whites, beaten stiff
1 t. baking powder
½ pt. whipping cream
1 t. vanilla
1 c. sugar
1 c. pecans, chopped

FRUIT CRUNCH

In 8-by-8-by-2-inch (1¼ quart) baking dish, combine pie filling and lemon juice. In medium-sized mixing bowl, beat margarine and sugar till well blended. Stir in flour, cinnamon, and granola. Sprinkle evenly over pie filling. Bake at 350° about 25 minutes or until bubbly and topping is golden brown. Serve warm or cool with ice cream or whipped topping.

–Mrs. Larry Henderson (Donna)

1 t. lemon juice
¼ c. softened margarine
¼ c. firmly packed brown sugar
⅓ c. all-purpose flour
1 (21 oz.) can pie filling (cherry, apple, or blueberry)
¼ t. cinnamon
½ granola

FROZEN DESSERT (Serves 8)

Fold together until mixed well. Freeze in airtight 8-by-12-inch container. Can be kept frozen and used as needed.

–Mrs. W. D. Stogner

1 can cherry pie filling
1 can condensed milk
1 large carton Cool Whip
1 can coconut
1 tall can pineapple tidbits
1 c. chopped pecans

GRANDMA'S PEACH COBBLER (Serves 8-10)

Stir milk, flour, ½ cup sugar, and melted margarine into baking dish greased with margarine. Pour fruit over top of mixture, stir in. Then sprinkle ½ cup sugar over top and bake at 425° for 30 minutes.

–Mrs. Jonathan Peterson (Murfi)

1 c. milk
1 c. sugar
1 can sliced peaches
½ c. flour
½ stick margarine (melted)

PEACH COBBLER (Serves 6-8)

Pour flour and sugar over peaches and mix in baking dish. Cut one stick of oleo into pieces and distribute over peaches.

9 peaches, cooked until tender
2 T. flour
1¾ c. sugar
dash of salt

Pastry:

Cut shortening into flour; add milk. Roll on floured board. Cut in pieces and put on top of peaches. Melt ½ stick of oleo; pour over top and sprinkle with sugar. Bake at 350° for 30 minutes. Serve hot with ice cream.

–Mrs. Billy K. Smith (Irlene)

1 c. flour
4 T. milk
⅓ c. shortening

QUICK FRUIT COBBLER (Serves 4-6)

Melt butter. Mix all other ingredients except fruit to make a smooth batter. Pour batter over butter. Do *not* stir. Add fruit and juice. Place in 350° oven for about 35-40 minutes or until brown.

–Mrs. George L. Tumlin, Jr. (Lynda)

¼ lb. margarine
1 c. sugar
2½ c. sweetened fruit (apples, peaches, etc.)
1 c. self-rising flour
⅔ c. milk

STRAWBERRY FLUFF (Serves 6-8)

Crust and mix ingredients and place on a cookie sheet and bake at 350° until brown. Crumble with folk as it bakes.

1 stick margarine, melted
¼ c. nuts
¼ c. brown sugar
1 c. flour

Filling:

Beat full 15 minutes. Do not underbeat. Fold in 1 carton whipped cream. Place ¾ crumb mixture in a pyrex (oblong) dish. Place strawberry mixture in and sprinkle remaining crumbs on top. Freeze until desired.

–Mrs. Bill Rogers

1 (10 oz.) box defrosted strawberries
2 T. lemon juice
⅔ c. sugar
2 egg whites

STRAWBERRY REFRIGERATOR DESSERT (Serves 8-10)

Combine strawberry jello dissolved in hot water, the angel food cake, and the strawberries. Pour over vanilla ice cream spread in 13-by-9-inch sheet pan and refrigerate for several hours.

–Mrs Stephen Glass (Jennifer)

1 (3 oz.) pkg. strawberry jello
1 c. hot water
1 angel food cake, cut in chunks
1 pkg. frozen strawberries (or 1½ c. fresh sliced)
2 c. vanilla ice cream

TORTONI SQUARES (Serves 8-10)

Combine almonds, butter, crumbs, extract. Mix well. Line dish with crumbs, saving 2 tablespoons for the top. Spoon half of the ice milk over the crumbs, making it level, and return to the freezer until firm. Then add half of the preserves, spreading evenly. Repeat, adding one more layer of each. Top with crumbs and freeze. Cut in squares to serve.

–Mrs. James Taylor (Maidee)

1 c. chopped toasted almonds
1 c. vanilla wafer crumbs
2 pt. vanilla ice milk (soft)
3 T. melted butter
1 t. almond extract
1 (12 oz.) jar apricot preserves

EDNA BROWN'S BANANA PUDDING (Serves 8)

Place half the vanilla wafers in a 2-quart ovenproof dish. Slice bananas over the wafers; add remaining wafers. Combine evaporated milk, whole milk, eggs, flour, salt, sugar, and vanilla together. Cook over medium heat until thick, stirring constantly. Remove from heat; stir in vanilla. Pour over bananas and vanilla wafers while hot.

1½ boxes vanilla wafers
3 or 4 large bananas
1 c. evaporated milk
1½ c. whole milk
4 eggs (separated)
3 T. flour
1 c. sugar
1 t. vanilla
dash salt

Topping:

Fold sugar into egg whites and add vanilla. Spread over pudding and brown lightly. Cool before serving.

–Mrs. James B. Brown (Edna)

4 egg whites, beaten stiff
½ T. vanilla
¾ c. sugar

HOLIDAY ICE CREAM (Serves 10)

Mix all ingredients together, return to freezer in covered container to harden. Serve in sherbet dishes. *–Mrs. James Richardson*

½ gal. vanilla ice cream, softened
1 c. toasted pecans, coarsely chopped
1 medium jar maraschino cherries, chopped
1 box coconut almond macaroons, crumbled

MANDY'S VANILLA ICE CREAM (Makes 1 gallon)

Mix together first four ingredients and add remaining. Can be made in ice cream freezer or frozen in trays in the refrigerator. Makes a freezerful. *–Mrs. Tom Mills (Leslie)*

1½ c. sugar
6 eggs
2 large cans evaporated milk
dash salt
3 T. vanilla
½ gal. milk

CHOCOLATE SAUCE

Place ingredients in a double boiler. Cook until thick. Serve warm over vanilla ice cream balls that are covered with nuts.

–Mrs. Bill Rogers (Luwilda)

1 stick oleo, melted
3 c. sugar
4 oz. semi-sweet chocolate
1 tall can evaporated milk

TRICOLORED ICES

Make sherbet or use commercial sherbet in three colors (orange, lime, raspberry). Line muffin pans with paper muffin pan liners. Using melon ball scoop, fill cups with assorted sherbet; top with teaspoon of whipped cream. Freeze until firm.

–Mrs. Fred Moseley (Gay)

APPLE COBBLER CAKE (Serves 15-20)

Blend first four ingredients together. Sift together and then mix gradually with next three ingredients. Fold in 1 cup chopped pecans and 3 cups chopped fresh apples (do not peel). Pour into well-greased and floured tube or Bundt pan. Bake in 350° oven for 1 hour.

1½ c. vegetable oil
3 eggs
2 c. sugar
2 t. vanilla
3 c. cake flour
½ t. salt
1 t. soda

Topping:

Pour over hot cake and let stand for one hour before removing from pan.

–Mrs. Tommy Kinchen (Ruth Ann)

¼ c. milk
1 stick butter
1 c. brown sugar

APPLE CAKE

Combine oil, eggs, and sugar. Mix well. Add flour and heat thoroughly. Add remaining ingredients and pour into flat greased pan. Bake at 350° 40-45 minutes.

–Mrs. Gary P. Hadden (Marilyn)

1 c. light vegetable oil
3 eggs
2 c. sugar
2 c. self-rising flour
1 c. pecans
1 t. cinnamon
1 t. vanilla
3 c. (5 or 6) apples, chopped
1 t. nutmeg

DOODLE CAKE (Serves 20)

Mix all ingredients just well enough to mix eggs. Pour into greased and floured 9-by-13-inch pan. Put cake into oven and set at 350° (*do not preheat oven*). Bake 40-45 minutes.

2 c. all-purpose flour
2 c. sugar
2 eggs
2 t. baking powder
⅛ t. salt
1 (20 oz.) can crushed pineapple, undrained

Topping:

Boil 3 minutes, then add chopped pecans or coconut. Pour over hot cake. Prick top of cake in several places to let filling seep in.
–Mrs. Chester Vaughn (Evelyn)

1 c. sugar
1 stick margarine
1 small can evaporated milk
1 c. chopped pecans (or coconut)

NEW SOCK-IT-TO-ME CAKE (Serves 12)

Mix all of the above. Pour half the batter into greased and floured Bundt pan. Sprinkle with 2 tablespoons brown sugar and 1 tablespoon cinnamon, mixed. Pour in remaining batter. Bake in 325° oven.
–The Committee

1 pkg. golden butter cake mix
1 t. vanilla
4 eggs (add one at a time)
½ pt. sour cream
¾ c. shortening
½ c. sugar
1 c. pecans

BANANA SPLIT CAKE (Serves 12)

Combine ½ cup margarine and graham cracker crumbs; pat firmly into a 9-by-13-inch pan. Combine 1 cup margarine, eggs, and sugar; beat 15 minutes; spread filling on crust. Slice bananas over filling. Sprinkle pineapple over bananas. Top with Cool Whip. Garnish with cherries and nuts. Refrigerate 3 hours before serving. Cut into squares and serve.
–Mrs. Paul Robertson (Judy)

1½ c. margarine
2 c. graham cracker crumbs
2 eggs
1 box confectioner's sugar
5 bananas
1 large can crushed pineapple, well drained
1 large carton Cool Whip
chopped cherries and nuts for garnish

BANANA SPLIT SUPREME (Serves 8-12)

Mix crushed wafers and 1 stick of melted oleo for crust in 9-by-13-inch pan. Combine 2 sticks oleo, sugar, eggs. Beat on low speed of mixer for 15 full minutes. Pour over crust. Add bananas and then pineapple and Cool Whip. Then sprinkle with cherries and pecans. *–Mrs. Ron McCaskill (Fran)*

1 box vanilla wafers, crushed
1 (20 oz.) can crushed pineapple, drained
½ c. chopped cherries
2 c. confectioner's sugar
3 sticks oleo, melted
2 eggs
1 large carton Cool Whip
½ c. chopped nuts
5 bananas, sliced

APRICOT NECTAR CAKE (Serves 12)

Mix all ingredients together except 3 tablespoons of apricot nectar. Bake at 350° for 50

1 box orange supreme cake mix
½ c. light vegetable oil

minutes. Glaze: 1 cup confectioner's sugar inches apart on an ungreased cookie sheet.

–Mrs. Jason Lee (Carolyn)

½ c. sugar
4 eggs
1 c. apricot nectar

BABY FOOD CAKE (Serves 12)

Sift dry ingredients together. Add cooking oil and eggs, one at a time, and mix well. Add plums and apricots; mix well. Add nuts last and bake in a tube or Bundt pan at 325° for 1 hour. *–Mrs. Lawrence Goff (Linda)*

2 c. sifted self-rising flour
½ t. salt
1 t. cloves
3 eggs
1 (4 oz.) jar apricot baby food
2 c. sugar
1 t. cinnamon
¾ c. cooking oil
1 (4 oz.) jar plum baby food
1 c. finely chopped nuts (opt.)

BUTTERMILK CAKE (Serves 16-20)

Cream the shortening and sugar. Add eggs, one at a time. Add flour. Add soda to hot water, then to buttermilk; then add to flour mixture. Add flavoring. Beat well. Bake in a tube or Bundt pan at 325° for about 1½ hours or 1¼ hours. Be sure to judge your ovens, as they vary.

–Mrs. Francis Sylvest, Sr.

1½ c. shortening
2½ c. sugar
4 eggs
3½ c. flour, plain or cake
½ t. soda
1 T. hot water
1 c. buttermilk
1 T. lemon or vanilla flavoring

MILLION-DOLLAR POUND CAKE (Serves 12)

Cream butter and butter flavoring. Add sugar gradually and cream well. Add eggs one at a time, mixing well after each addition. Sift flour 4 times. Add flour and milk alternately in small amounts. Bake 1 hour and 35 minutes at 325° in tube pan. Wrap in foil while still hot.

–Mrs. John McPherson (Marie)

1 T. butter
3 c. sugar
6 eggs
½ t. almond extract
1 t. butter flavoring
¾ c. sweet milk
4 c. flour
1 t. vanilla extract

COCONUT POUND CAKE (Serves 12)

Beat shortening and sugar on high speed 10 minutes. Add eggs one at a time. Add dry ingredients alternately with milk. Fold in

1½ c. shortening
2½ c. sugar
5 eggs
3 c. flour

coconut and flavoring. Bake in tube; put in cold oven. Bake at 350° for 1¾ hours.

1 t. baking powder
¼ t. salt
1 c. sweet milk
1 box flaked coconut
2 t. coconut flavoring

Sauce:

Boil 5 minutes; pour over cake while hot.

–Mrs. Edna Brown

2 c. sugar
3 T. butter
¼ c. white Karo syrup
1 c. water
2 T. coconut flavoring

POUND CAKE (Serves 12)

Mix as you would any cake. Pour in tube pan. Start in a *cold* oven; turn to 300° and bake for 1½ hours. Do not open oven door for at least 1 hour.

½ c. shortening
2 sticks butter
3 c. sugar
3 c. flour
½ t. baking powder
5 eggs
1 c. evaporated milk
1 t. vanilla or almond flavoring
1 t. lemon flavoring

Lemon Glaze:

Pour on warm cake as soon as taken from oven. Let cool. Then remove from pan.

–Mrs. J. Wash Watta (Mattie Leila)

1 c. confectioner's sugar
1 lemon (juice)
½ stick melted oleo

CREAM CHEESE POUND CAKE (Serves 12)

Cream butter, cream cheese, sugar and vanilla. Add flour and eggs alternately. Bake at 300° for 1½ hours.

–Mrs. Paul Robertson (Judy)
Mrs. Bob Golden (Mary)
Mrs. Joe B. Nesom (Janice)

3 sticks butter or oleo
1 (8 oz.) pkg. cream cheese
3 c. sugar
1½ t. vanilla
3 c. cake flour
6 eggs

SOUR CREAM POUND CAKE (Serves 12)

Sift flour and dry ingredients together. Cream butter and sugar; add eggs, one at a time; cream thoroughly. Add sour cream and mix well. Blend in dry ingredients; add van-

2 sticks butter
6 eggs
3 c. plain white flour, sifted
1 t. vanilla
3 c. sugar

illa. Pour into greased pan (with wax paper lining). Preheat oven to 325°. Bake 1½ hours.

–Mrs. Edwin Quattlebaum (Betty W.)
Mrs. Hugh Tobias (Marie)

1 c. sour cream
¼ t. soda

MISSISSIPPI POUND CAKE (Serves 12)

Mix salt and baking powder with flour. Cream margarine and sugar. Add eggs one at a time, beating well after each addition. Add flour, a little at a time, stirring or folding. Add flavoring. Bake in a tube pan at 325° for 1 hour.

–Mrs. Roy McKay (Marcia)

1 c. butter or margarine
5 large or 6 small eggs
1 t. desired flavoring
½ t. salt
2 c. sugar
2 c. flour, plain
1 t. baking powder

POUND CAKE (Serves 12)

Cream shortening, margarine, and sugar. Add eggs one at a time, beating after each egg. Sift flour, salt, and baking powder together. Add to sugar mixture, alternating with milk. Add vanilla. Pour in a greased tube pan. Bake at 325° 1½-2 hours. Insert toothpick to test doneness. Cool 10 minutes. Remove from pan. NOTE: This cake gets better the third day after baking. Will keep about 1 week before getting stale if kept in airtight container.

–Mrs. Morris Murray, Jr. (Brenda)

1 c. shortening
1 stick margarine
3 c. sugar
½ t. baking powder
½ t. salt
1 c. milk
1½ t. vanilla
6 eggs
3 c. all-purpose plain flour

FOUR-FLAVOR POUND CAKE (Serves 12)

Cream sugar and shortening; add eggs one at a time and beat after each addition. Sift dry ingredients together and add (alternately with milk) to sugar and shortening mixture. Pour into greased and floured pan. Bake at 350° for 1¼ hours. (If oven is exceedingly hot, reduce heat to 300° or 325° and watch.) *–Mrs. Ron Albright (Jeanette)*

3 c. sugar
1 c. shortening
1 c. milk
5 whole eggs
1 t. lemon extract
1 t. butter extract
3 c. flour
½ t. salt
1 t. baking powder, level
1 t. vanilla extract
1 t. orange extract

CHOCOLATE POUND CAKE (Serves 12)

Cream butter and sugar. Beat eggs with butter until light and fluffy. Sift all dry ingredients together. Add flour mixture (alternating with milk) to butter and eggs, always beginning and ending with flour. Bake in large tube pan or two loaf pans. Bake at 325° 1¼ hours. *–Miss Sandi Swartz*

½ lb. butter (or margarine)
½ c. shortening
3 c. sugar
5 eggs
3 c. cake flour or 2½ c. plus 2 T. all-purpose flour
½ t. baking powder
½ t. salt
1 c. milk
4 heaping T. cocoa
1 T. vanilla

7-POUND CAKE (Serves 12)

Cream oleo, shortening, sugar and eggs. Add flour slowly. Blend with remaining ingredients. Bake in oven at 300° for 1½ hours.
–Mrs. W. David Ivy (O'Hara)

2 sticks oleo
5 eggs
3 c. plain flour
2 t. extract (your choice)
½ c. shortening
3 c. sugar
1 small bottle 7-Up (¾ c.)

ANN'S SOUR CREAM COFFEE CAKE (Serves 12)

Cream oleo; add sugar and eggs, and beat. Fold in sour cream and vanilla. Fold in flour, baking powder, and salt. Pour half of batter in greased loaf pan.

2 sticks oleo
2 c. sugar
2 eggs
1 c. sour cream
1 t. vanilla
2 c. flour
¼ t. salt
1 t. baking powder

Mix together:

Sprinkle half of this mixture on top of batter. Add remaining batter and top with other half of mixture. Bake at 350° for 1 hour.
–Mrs. John McPherson (Marie)

½ c. chopped nuts
½ c. brown sugar
1 t. cinnamon

PUMPKIN CAKE (Serves 12)

Mix all ingredients together at one time (no need to sift). Use either 13-by-9-inch oblong pan or 2-by-8-inch round pans.

2 c. flour
2 t. cinnamon
½ t. salt
1 c. cooking oil
2 c. pumpkin
2 t. baking soda
1 t. baking powder
2 c. sugar
4 eggs

Frosting:

Use mixer to combine first four ingredients. Stir in nuts. *–Mrs. James Bradfield (Paula)*

1 stick butter or margarine
1 box confectioner's sugar
½ c. chopped nuts
1 (8 oz.) pkg. cream cheese
2 t. vanilla

CHOCOLATE SHEET CAKE (Serves 12-16)

Sift together sugar and flour. Place water and margarine, shortening, cocoa, and salt in saucepan. Bring to boil, stirring constantly. Add to flour mixture and beat by hand until smooth. Add eggs, one at a time, beating until smooth. Then add buttermilk with soda dissolved in it and vanilla. Bake 25-30 minutes in 350° oven (325° if Pyrex baking dish is used). Spread icing on hot cake. *–Mrs. George C. Herndon (Claire)*
Mrs. Francis Sylvest, Sr.
Mrs. David H. Sandifer (Jackie)
Mrs. Irlene Smith

2 c. sugar
1 stick margarine
1 c. water
2 T. cocoa
½ c. buttermilk
1 t. vanilla
2 c. flour
½ c. shortening
½ t. salt
2 eggs
1 t. soda

Icing:
1 stick margarine
6 T. milk
1 t. vanilla
1 box confectioner's sugar
½-1 c. pecans
3 T. cocoa or 1 sq. unsweetened baking chocolate

CHOCOLATE SYRUP CAKE (Serves 10-12)

Cream together and add: 1 c. flour and 1 large can chocolate syrup. Bake for 30 minutes at 350° in a 9-by-13-inch pan. Do not overcook.

1 stick butter
4 eggs
1 c. sugar

Frosting:

Mix the above and smooth over cake while still warm. Then put the cake in the refrigerator with a cover and store until ready to cut in squares and serve.
–Mrs. Christopher Barbee (Brenda)

1 stick butter
1 t. vanilla
1 box confectioner's sugar

CHOCOLATE CAKE (Serves 12)

Chip chocolate squares and pour boiling water over them. Sift dry ingredients and

2½ sq. unsweetened chocolate
¾ c. boiling water
1¾ c. sifted flour

add to chocolate and water. Drop in shortening and vanilla. Beat 2 minutes on low and add eggs and milk. Beat 2 minutes more on low speed. Bake in 2 layers or in 13-by-9-by-2-inch pan. Layers: 25-30 minutes at 350°. Sheet cake: 45-50 minutes at 350°.

¾ t. soda
1½ c. sugar
½ t. baking powder
¾ t. salt
½ c. shortening
1 t. vanilla
2 eggs
⅓ c. buttermilk

Icing:

Put chocolate, margarine, and shortening in top of double boiler and melt. Add all other ingredients except vanilla. Bring to rapid boil and cook until a small amount dropped in cold water forms a soft ball. Cool slightly. Add vanilla and beat until right consistency to spread on cake. Add nuts if desired.

–Mrs. Dan Ireland (Polly)

3 oz. unsweetened chocolate, cut fine
4 T. margarine
4 T. shortening
3 c. sugar
1 c. milk
2 T. white corn syrup
1 t. vanilla
nuts (optional)

COCONUT CAKE (Serves 12)

1 box butter cake mix, prepared with milk instead of water. Bake in 4 layers.

Filling:

Mix sugar and sour cream and then coconut. Spread between all the layers.

–Mrs. Tony Hendrix (Marie)

2 c. sugar
1 (8 oz.) pkg. sour cream
2 (6 oz.) pkg, frozen coconut

SAD CAKE (Serves 12)

Mix all ingredients together. Bake in greased 13-by-8-inch pan at 365° for 30 minutes. Allow cake to cool and slice in 1-inch squares. *–Mrs. Carl Wilks, Jr.*

4 eggs
1 (6 or 6½ oz.) pkg. biscuit mix
½-1 c. pecans (optional)
1 lb. brown sugar
1 (6 oz.) pkg. chocolate chips

A GOOD CAKE (Serves 12)

Beat all ingredients together including juice from oranges. Bake in layers.

1 pkg. butter cake mix
4 eggs
½ c. light vegetable oil
1 can mandarin oranges

Icing:

Mix all ingredients together until smooth. Spread between cake layers and on top. Let stand in refrigerator until chilled.

–Mrs. Julian Stephens, Jr. (Tamara)

1 (9 oz.) carton Cool Whip
1 large can crushed pineapple, undrained
1 pkg. vanilla instant pudding

MISSISSIPPI MUD CAKE (Serves 12)

Melt butter and chocolate together. Cream sugar and eggs. Add remaining ingredients. Pour into 13-by-9-inch greased and floured pan. Bake at 350° for 45 minutes. While cake is still hot, punch holes in cake. Spread marshmallow cream on top.

1 c. butter or oleo
⅓ c. cocoa
2 c. sugar
4 eggs
1 jar marshmallow cream
1½ c. flour
pinch of salt
1½ c. chopped nuts
1 t. vanilla

Icing:

Mix and heat and pour over the marshmallow cream. *–Mrs. Ron Albright (Jeanette)*

¼ c. butter or oleo
⅓ c. cocoa
1 t. vanilla
1 box confectioner's sugar
⅓ c. milk

SCRIPTURE CAKE (Serves 12)

Cream butter with sugar. Chop figs and add to mixture. Beat eggs until frothy and add milk. Sift part of flour with baking powder; add remaining flour. Add alternately to creamed mixture with egg mixture. Beat well. Add honey. Chop raisins and almonds: add to mix with remaining ingredients. Mix well. Pour into tube pan and bake at 375° for 30 minutes. Test. May require 15 minutes more. *–Mrs. Steve Wallace (Janet)*

1 c. Judges 5:25
2 c. Jeremiah 6:20
2 c. Nahum 3:12
6 Isaiah 10:14
½ c. Judges 4:19
4 c. Kings 4:22
2 T. Amos 4:25
2 T. I Samuel 14:25
2 c. I Samuel 30:12
2 c. Numbers 17:8
Pinch of Leviticus 2:13
II Chronicles to taste

EAGLE BRAND FRUITCAKE (Serves 16-20)

Mix all ingredients together. Pour into tube pan that has been well greased and lined with wax paper. Cook about 1½ hours at 300° or until it is a light brown.

–Mrs. Robin Arflin

1 qt. chopped nuts
1 lb. candied cherries, red and green
1 large pkg. dates, chopped
2 cans Eagle Brand milk
1 lb. candied pineapple, red and green
1 large pkg. flaked coconut

ITALIAN CREAM CAKE (Serves 12)

Cream sugar, shortening, and oleo, adding 5 egg yolks. Add soda to buttermilk and combine alternately with flour. Add vanilla and coconut. Fold in stiffly beaten egg whites. Bake at 350-375° for 35-40 minutes in 3 layers, or 25 minutes in sheet pan.

2 c. sugar
½ c. shortening
1 stick oleo
1 t. soda
1 c. buttermilk
2 c. flour
1 t. vanilla
1 pkg. fresh frozen coconut

Icing:

Combine cream cheese and oleo. Add remaining ingredients and spread on cake.

–Mrs. Billy Simmons (Flo)

1 (8 oz.) pkg. cream cheese
1 stick oleo
1 box confectioner's sugar
1 t. vanilla
1 c. pecans, finely chopped

FRUIT COCKTAIL CAKE (Serves 12)

Mix the above ingredients. Pour into a baking pan. Sprinkle with 1 cup brown sugar and 1 cup chopped pecans. Bake at 350° for 35 minutes.

2 c. self-rising flour
2 eggs, beaten
1½ c. sugar
1 (16 oz.) can fruit cocktail, undrained

Topping:

Boil ingredients 5 minutes, then add one can flaked coconut and 1 teaspoon vanilla. Pour this mixture over cake while hot. Serve it hot or save it; it gets better.

–Mrs. Thomas Haynes (Gloria)

¾ c. white sugar
1 stick margarine
½ c. evaporated milk

PRALINE CAKE (Serves 12)

Warm buttermilk and margarine in a saucepan until margarine is melted; add brown sugar and stir until dissolved. Pour into mixing bowl; add eggs and beat well. Add other dry ingredients sifted together. Beat and add vanilla. Bake in a greased, floured pan, 14 by 9 by 2 inches at 350° for 35-50 minutes. (Do not remove from pan.)

1 c. buttermilk
1 stick margarine
2 c. light brown sugar
2 eggs
2 c. flour
2 heaping T. cocoa
1 t. soda
1 T. vanilla

Topping:

In a small saucepan mix evaporated milk, margarine, brown sugar, and nuts. Warm until margarine and sugar are dissolved and spread over cake. Place cake under broiler until topping bubbles (about 5 minutes) and watch very closely or it will burn.

–Mrs. Melvin J. Poole (Linda)

6 T. evaporated milk
1 stick margarine
1 c. light brown sugar
1 c. nuts

ORANGE CANDY CAKE (Serves 12)

Cream butter with granulated sugar. Add eggs one at a time, creaming well after each addition. Dissolve soda in buttermilk, then alternately add to creamed mixture with 3½ cups of the flour. Mix remaining ½ cup flour with dates, candy pieces, and chopped nuts. Add to batter with coconut. Pour batter into 10-inch tube pan that has been greased and floured on bottom and sides. Bake at 250° for 3 hours or until cake springs back when lightly pressed. Meanwhile, combine orange juice and confectioner's sugar; mix well. Immediately pour over hot cake in pan. Let stand overnight in pan; then remove from pan and slice to serve. NOTE: Cake may be wrapped in plastic wrap and stored in refrigerator for about 2 weeks.

–Mrs. (Maurine Austin) Dudley

1 c. butter or oleo
2 c. sugar
4 eggs
1 t. baking soda
1 c. buttermilk
1 lb. orange candy slices, cut into small pieces
1 c. flaked coconut
4 c. unsifted all-purpose flour
1 (14 oz.) box dates, cut into small pieces
2 c. chopped nuts
1 c. reconstituted frozen or fresh orange juice
1 c. unsifted confectioner's sugar

SPICY OATMEAL CAKE (Serves 12)

Pour boiling water over oats; cover and let stand 20 minutes. Beat butter until creamy; beat in sugars, vanilla, and eggs. Add oats mixture; mix well. Sift together flour, soda, salt, cinnamon, and nutmeg. Add to creamed mixture, mixing well. Pour batter into well greased and floured 12¾-by-9-inch pan. Bake in preheated 350° oven for 45-50 minutes. Leave cake in pan.

2 c. boiling water
1½ c. oats (quick or old-fashioned, uncooked)
1 c. granulated sugar
2 c. firmly packed brown sugar
1½ t. vanilla
3 eggs
2¼ c. sifted all-purpose flour
1 t. soda
1 t. salt
1 t. cinnamon
½ t. nutmeg
⅔ c. butter or margarine

Cream Cheese Frosting:

Allow cream cheese and butter to soften. Combine all ingredients. Spread on cooled cake. *–Mrs. J. H. Dieter*

½ c. butter or margarine
1 box confectioner's sugar
1 (8 oz.) pkg. cream cheese

NEVER-FAIL PIE CRUST

Blend dry ingredients with shortening; add egg and liquids. Form into 3 or 4 balls. Wrap in wax paper. Store in refrigerator or freeze. Take out a roll as needed; warm to room temperature. Roll on heavily floured board. Place in the plate; flute edge with fingers, fork or spoon. Prick bottom of crust with fork and mash sides with fork before baking 10-12 minutes in 425° oven.
–Mrs. Mack P. Jones (Marie Martin)

3 c. flour
1 t. baking powder
1 t. salt
⅓ c. shortening
1 egg
5 T. water
1 T. vinegar

CRUSTS FOR PIES

Mix first 3 ingredients together. Cut in butter. Add ice water. Place on lightly floured board. Roll out into 2 pie crusts. The less you work with the dough, the crisper the crust.
–Mrs. Virginia Joyner

2¼ c. flour
⅔ c. shortening
1 t. salt
½ stick butter
5 T. ice water

CHOCOLATE ALMOND PIE (Serves 8)

Melt candy, marshmallows, and milk together over hot water. Cool. Fold in whipped cream or topping. Pour in baked shell. Chill well. *–Mrs. Ray Rust (Joy)*

1 (7½ oz.) chocolate bar with almonds
18 large marshmallows
½ c. milk
½ pt. whipping cream or prepared whipped topping
9-inch baked pie crust

AUNT EZMA'S CHOCOLATE PIE (Serves 6)

Combine sugar, flour, cocoa, and salt in the top of a double boiler. Beat eggs and milk until frothy and add to the dry mixture. Cook until thickened, add butter and van-

1½ c. sugar
½ c. flour
½ c. cocoa
dash of salt
3 egg yolks

illa. Place in baked 9-inch pastry shell; add meringue and brown.

–Mrs. Thomas Moody (Melba)

2 c. milk
1 T. butter
1 t. vanilla

CHOCOLATE PIE (Serves 8)

Mix all ingredients and pour into unbaked pie shell. Bake at 350° for 30-35 minutes or until center is firm.

–Mrs. Dan Ireland (Polly)

½ stick margarine, melted
½ c. evaporated milk
1½ c. sugar
1 t. vanilla
3 T. cocoa
2 eggs
1 unbaked pie shell

MY FAVORITE CHOCOLATE PIE

Mix flour, sugar, and salt; gradually add scalded milk that has had 2 (1 oz.) squares unsweetened chocolate melted in it. Cook over moderate heat, stirring constantly until mixture thickens and boils. Cook 2 minutes; remove from heat. Add small amount to egg yolks; stir into remaining hot mixture; cook 1 minute, stirring constantly. Add butter and vanilla; cool slightly. Pour into baked pastry shell. Cool. Cover with meringue and bake in 350° oven for 12-15 minutes. After cooled, cover and store in the refrigerator.

–Mrs. Mack Jones (Marie Martin)

⅓ cup sifted flour
1 c. sugar
¼ t. salt
2 c. milk, scalded
3 slightly beaten egg yolks
2 T. butter or margarine
½ t. vanilla
1 baked 9-inch or 8-inch pie shell
2 (1 oz.) square unsweetened chocolate

SWEET POTATO PIE (Serves 8)

Place mashed sweet potatoes in mixing bowl; add sugar, cinnamon, nutmeg, and salt. Beat with rotary beater or electric mixer until blended. Add eggs, milk, and melted butter and beat until fluffy. Pour into a prepared 9-inch pastry shell. Bake 50-60 minutes or until a knife inserted in center comes lean. If desired, serve with whipped cream sprinkled with chopped pecans.

–Mrs. William P. Tuck

2 c. mashed, cooked sweet potatoes
¾ c. sugar
1 t. cinnamon
½ t. nutmeg
½ t. salt
3 eggs, slightly beaten
1 c. milk, scalded
2 T. melted butter or margarine

AUNT BERT'S SURPRISE PIE (Serves 8)

Bake crust and when cool press into the bottom a mixture of brown sugar and butter. Sprinkle with pecans and then add pie filling cooked as package directs. When ready to serve, cover with cool whip.

–Mrs. Tony Hendrix (Marie)

1 large pie crust baked
½ c. brown sugar
½ c. butter
½ c. pecans
1 box lemon pie filling

MILLION-DOLLAR PIE (Makes 2 pies)

Mix together in this order: milk, lemon juice, Cool Whip, coconut, crushed pineapple, and pecans. Pour into baked pie shells.

–Mrs. Wayne Hoggle (Romie)

1 can sweetened condensed milk
¼ c. lemon juice
1 (9 oz.) carton Cool Whip
1 c. flaked coconut
1 small can crushed pineapple, drained
1 c. chopped pecans

IMPOSSIBLE PIE (Serves 8)

Blend first two ingredients then add remaining. Bake at 350° in a 10-inch well greased pyrex pie dish for 45-50 minutes.

–Mrs. Francis Sylvest, Sr.

4 T. butter or margarine
½ c. sugar
4 eggs (one at a time)
1 t. vanilla
1 c. coconut
2 c. milk
½ c. Bisquick

LEMON PECAN PIE (Serves 8)

Mix the ingredients in the order given, but do not use a mixer or beat until frothy. Pour into 8-inch unbaked pie shell. Put in preheated 400° oven and bake about 10 minutes. Reduce oven temperature to 325° and bake for another 40-45 minutes.

(For variety try Orange Pecan Pie. Substitute fresh orange juice for lemon juice and add 1 teaspoon orange extract in place of lemon extract.)

–Mrs. Ron Meyer

3 eggs
⅓ stick of oleo, melted (do not use whipped oleo)
1 t. lemon extract
1½ c. white sugar
¾ c. pecans (halves or pieces)
juice of ½ lemon (⅛ c.)

LEMON MERINGUE PIE (Serves 8)

Bake and cool pastry. In a saucepan combine the sugar, flour, cornstarch, and salt. Stir in

1 (9-inch) baked pastry shell
1 c. sugar

water. Cook and stir over medium heat until thickened and clear. Add a little hot mixture to egg yolks; return all to hot mixture. Cook one minute longer, stirring constantly. Remove from fire. Blend in butter, lemon juice, and lemon peel. Pour mixture into pastry shell. Make a meringue of the egg whites and 6 tablespoons sugar. Beat egg whites until soft peaks form; gradually add the sugar. Beat to stiff peaks. Spread over hot filling. Bake at 425° for 5 minutes, until brown. *–Mrs. Francis Sylvest, Sr.*

¼ c. flour, plain
3 T. cornstarch
¼ t. salt
2 c. water
3 egg yolks, beaten
1 T. butter or margarine
¼ c. lemon juice
1 t. lemon peel, grated
3 egg whites
6 T. sugar

LIME CHIFFON PIE (Serves 8)

Mix milk and limeade concentrate until well blended. Then add whipped topping and fold into mixture. Add green food coloring until a light lime green color is achieved. Pour into cooked pie crust. Refrigerate at least 3 hours prior to serving. *–Mrs. Dan Storey (Dale)*

1 can sweetened condensed milk
1 (9 oz.) carton whipped topping
2-4 drops green food coloring
1 can defrosted limeade concentrate

ICE CREAM PIE (Serves 8)

Soften ice cream for about 20 minutes. Place in pie shell. Freeze one hour. Add topping. Garnish with nuts. Store in freezer until 10 minutes before serving.

–Mrs. Steve Wallace (Janet)

1 qt. vanilla ice cream
1 graham cracker pie shell
1 jar fudge topping for ice cream
½ c. pecans or walnuts

BANANA-BLUEBERRY CHEESE PIE (Serves 6)

Blend cream cheese and sugar until light and fluffy. Set aside. Prepare Dream Whip according to directions. Blend with cream cheese mixture. Line a baked pie shell with thin-sliced bananas. Pour cream mixture over bananas; cover with ½ can blueberry pie filling. Before adding the rest of pie filling, mix in 1 tablespoon lemon juice and pour over pie. Chill about two hours before serving. *–Mrs. Stephen Glass (Jennifer)*

8 oz. cream cheese
1 c. confectioner's sugar
1 pkg. Dream Whip
1 baked pie shell
2 large bananas
½ can blueberry pie filling
1 T. lemon juice

NORWEGIAN APPLE PIE (Serves 8)

Mix the first two ingredients together well then add remaining ingredients. Pour in buttered pie plate and bake at 350° for 35 minutes. Top with whip cream.

–Mrs. Tim Dixon (Susan)

1½ c. sugar
2 eggs
pinch of salt
1 c. flour
½-1 c. chopped nuts
2 c. diced apples
1 t. almond or vanilla extract
2 t. baking powder

BROWN PAPER BAG APPLE PIE (Serves 6-8)

Put sliced, peeled, and cored apples in pie crust. Sprinkle cinnamon, sugar, and flour over apples. Place butter on top. Put second pie shell on top, pinching edges, and put holes in top. Place in paper bag and bake at 350° for 1 hour or until the crust is brown. Serve with ice cream.

–Mrs. Larry Henderson (Donna)

2 frozen pie shells
4-5 small green apples
1 t. cinnamon
1 c. sugar
2-3 T. flour
3-4 pats butter

BUTTERMILK PIE (Serves 8)

Beat eggs and sugar until light (do not use mixer). Melt oleo and pour into egg and sugar mixture. Add remaining ingredients and pour into pie crust. Cook in 350° oven for 1 hour. *–Mrs. Jonathan Pedersen (Murfi)*

3 eggs
2 c. sugar
½ stick oleo
½ t. vanilla
1 c. buttermilk
pinch of salt

DERBY PIE (Serves 8)

Mix all ingredients. Pour into unbaked pie shell. Bake in 350° oven for 1 hour. Do not overbake. *–Mrs. Hugh Tobias (Marie Rush)*

1 c. sugar
½ c. flour
2 eggs
1 stick melted butter
1 t. vanilla
1 c. pecans
1 c. chocolate chips

TOASTED COCONUT PECAN PIE (Serves 8)

Preheat oven to 350°. Thoroughly combine eggs, sugar, butter, lemon juice, and vanilla. Stir in coconut and nuts. Pour into pie shell. Bake for 45-50 minutes or until filling is set.

3 eggs, beaten
1½ c. sugar
½ c. butter or margarine, melted
2 t. lemon juice
1 t. vanilla

Cool. Garnish with sweetened whipped cream and pecan halves if desired.
–Mrs. Dennis Rogers (Judy)

1 can flaked coconut
½ c. coarsely chopped nuts
1 unbaked 9-inch pie shell

COCONUT CREAM PIE (Serves 8)

Beat egg yolks; add sugar, flour, and milk. Mix well. Cook over medium heat until thick. Remove from heat; add coconut and vanilla. Pour into baked pie shell. Beat egg whites until stiff and add 3 tablespoons of sugar. Pour onto pie filling; sprinkle with coconut. Bake until golden brown.
–Mrs. Billy K. Smith (Irlene)

2 eggs, separated
1 c. sugar
4 T. flour
2 c. milk
1 c. coconut
1 t. vanilla
3 T. sugar

COCONUT PIE (Serves 8)

Blend margarine, sugar, and eggs. Add vinegar, vanilla and coconut. Mix well. Turn into pie shell. Bake at 325° for 1 hour.
–Mrs. George L. Tumlin (Lynda)

1 stick margarine
1½ c. sugar
3 eggs
1 T. vinegar
1 t. vanilla
1 c. coconut
1 (9-inch) pie shell, unbaked

COCONUT ANGEL PIE (Serves 8)

Make a graham cracker crust. Bake until it seals good. Beat egg whites until frothy; add salt and vinegar; beat until real stiff, gradually adding sugar. Spread into crust; bake very slowly at about 200° until brown. Set aside and cool. This will take about an hour or two. Whip cream, 2 tablespoons sugar, and add can of coconut. Save one-quarter of coconut to toast and put that on top.
–The Committee

4 eggs (whites)
¼ t. salt
1 t. vinegar
1 c. sugar
½ pt. whipping cream
2 T. sugar
1 can coconut

LEMONADE PIE (Serves 8)

Mix in order given; pour into baked pie shell or small tarts. VARIATION: use pink lemonade and a few drops red food color or limeade and a few drops green food color. The ingredients

1 can sweetened condensed milk
1 small can lemonade concentrate
1 small carton whipped topping, thawed

can be kept on shelf and in freezer for unexpected company.

–The Committee

RITZ CRACKER PIE (Serves 8)

Beat egg whites until they form stiff peaks. Add baking powder, sugar, and nuts. Crush Ritz crackers (can be done in blender). Add to the above mixture. Pour in a pie pan. Bake at 350° for 25 minutes. *Time carefully.* Cool thoroughly. Top with chilled whipped cream and sprinkle with coconut.

–Miss Catherine Archer

3 egg whites
1 t. baking powder
1 c. sugar
1 c. chopped pecans
21 Ritz crackers
whipped cream or whipped topping mix
coconut

FRUIT PIZZA (Serves 8)

Cut dough into ⅛-inch slices. Line 14-inch pizza pan with slices. Bake at 375° for 12 minutes. Cool. Blend softened cream cheese, sugar, and vanilla. Spread over cookie crust. Arrange fruit over cream cheese layer. Glaze with preserves mixed with water and juice.

–Mrs. Raymond Garner (Donna)

1 roll refrigerated sugar cookie dough
1 (8 oz.) pkg. cream cheese
⅓ c. sugar
½ t. vanilla
any variety fresh fruit
marmalade, peach, or apricot preserves
¼ c. orange juice
1 t. water

STRAWBERRY PIE (Serves 8)

Boil cornstarch, sugar, and water until clear. Take off heat. Add jello. Stir. Let cool. Clean and slice strawberries. Add them to mixture. Pour into baked, cooled pie shell. Refrigerate until jellied.

–Miss Linda Ray

2 T. cornstarch
1 c. sugar
1 c. water
4 T. strawberry or lemon jello
1 pt. strawberries

STRAWBERRY PIE (Serves 8)

Cook sugar, cornstarch, and 7-Up until thick. Cool slightly. Add enough red food coloring to color. Spread berries in cooked pie shell and pour above mixture over berries. Chill. When ready to serve, top with whipped cream.

1 c. sugar
4 T. cornstarch
1 (10 oz.) bottle 7-Up
red food coloring
2 pt. fresh strawberries
whipped cream

Pie shell:

Form crust in plate. Bake until brown. Cool. Good for chocolate pie, strawberry pie, and so on.

–Mrs. Howard Alford (Kay)

1 stick butter
1 T. sugar
1 c. plain flour
1 c. chopped pecans

SWISS FRUIT PIE (Serves 10)

Sprinkle grated nuts over uncooked pastry shell. Pare and slice fresh fruit into shell. Bake in hot oven 20 minutes. Blend eggs, sugar, cinnamon and cream. Pour over hot, cooked fruit pie and bake 15 minutes more.

–Miss Vivian Holder

pastry shell
grated nuts
fruit in season (plums, pears, apples)
2 eggs
cinnamon
1 T. sugar
¼ c. cream

TEXAS PIE (Serves 8)

Mix ingredients well and pour into pie crust. Bake at 350° for 45 minutes.

–Mrs. Leroy Yarbrough (Edwyna)

2 c. sugar
4 eggs
1 T. flour
1 can flaked coconut
1 10-inch unbaked pie crust shell
1 stick butter, melted
1 T. cornmeal
1 t. vanilla
1 small can crushed pineapple, undrained

TRIPLE-FRUIT PIE (Serves 8)

Drain cherries and pineapple and add enough water to juice to make 1 cup liquid. Color pineapple and cherries with red food coloring. Stir juice into sugar and cornstarch; mix well. Add pineapple and cherries to mixture. Cook over medium heat until thick. Remove from heat; stir in vanilla and chill. When mixture is cooled, stir in diced bananas and pecans. Divide mixture and pour into 2 baked pie shells. Refrigerate until firm. Top with whipped cream before serving. *–Mrs. Charles Westbrook (Jane)*

1 c. sour, pitted (red tart) cherries (not pie filling)
1 small can pineapple, crushed
1 T. red food coloring
3½ T. cornstarch
1 T. vanilla extract
3 large bananas, diced
¾ c. chopped pecans
1 c. sugar
whipped cream

YUMMIE (Serves 6-8)

Mix Dream Whip according to directions on package. Add cream cheese (softened to room temperature) and whip for 3 minutes. Spread half of whipped mixture in the pie crust. Add the cherry pie filling and top with remaining Dream Whip. Chill pie for 2 hours. *–Mrs. Paul Hugger (Vickie)*

2 envelopes Dream Whip
1 (8 oz.) pkg. cream cheese
1 can cherry pie filling
1 graham cracker crust

THANKSGIVING PIE (Serves 8)

Cream butter, sugar, and flour together. Add whole eggs, yolks, and cottage cheese. Mixing well, add nutmeg, lemon juice, and rind. Add nuts and raisins. Stir until blended thoroughly. Pour into pastry shell and bake at 400° for 30-35 minutes or until done. *–Mrs. Paul Robertson (Judy)*

¼ c. butter or margarine
1¼ c. white sugar
2¼ t. plain flour
2 eggs
2 egg yolks
1 (4 oz.) carton cottage cheese
½ t. nutmeg
½ lemon (juice)
grate the rind of ½ lemon
⅓ c. chopped raisins
⅓ c. chopped pecans

NO-CRUST PIE (Serves 8)

Mix all ingredients and pour mixture into greased 10-inch pie plate. Bake at 300° 30-45 minutes. *–Mrs. Robert Neese (Beth)*

4 eggs
½ c. flour
1½ t. vanilla
1 small pkg. frozen coconut (optional)
1⅓ c. sugar
2 c. milk
2 T. margarine

APRICOT-COCONUT CONFECTION (Makes 5½ dozen)

Combine beaten eggs, sugar, and apricots in lightly buttered skillet. Cook over low heat. Mix with vanilla wafer crumbs. Stir in pecans and 1 can of coconut. Cool until easy to handle. Shape into 1-inch balls and roll in remaining coconut. Store in tightly covered box. *–Dr. Helen Falls*

3 eggs, beaten
8 oz. (1½ c.) dried apricots, chopped
about 2 c. finely rolled vanilla wafers
¾ c. chopped pecans
2 (3½ oz.) cans flaked coconut
½ c. sugar

BLOND BROWNIES (Serves 24)

Sift dry ingredients and add nuts. Melt butter and mix in brown sugar, egg, and vanilla. Add flour mixture to butter mixture and mix well. Spread in square baking pan and sprinkle chips on top. Bake at 350° for 25 minutes. Cut into squares. Can be doubled and is great for after-church fellowships.

–Mrs. Steve Wallace (Janet)

1 c. flour
½ T. baking powder
⅛ T. salt
⅛ T. soda
1 (6 oz.) bag chocolate chips
⅓ c. butter
1 c. brown sugar
1 egg, beaten
1 T. vanilla

BUTTER COOKIES (Makes 3 dozen)

Cream butter and sugar thoroughly; add unbeaten egg yolk and vanilla. Add flour gradually, mixing well. Form small balls of dough and indent centers with finger, pressing in deeply. Bake at 375° on ungreased cookie sheet. Do not brown. While still hot, fill hole in cookie with tart jelly.

–Mrs. Fred Moseley (Gay)

1 stick butter
1⅓ c. sugar
1 egg yolk
1 t. vanilla
1⅓ c. flour, sifted
tart jelly

BUTTERSCOTCH BROWNIES (Makes 16 squares)

Heat oven to 350°. Melt butter over low heat. Take from heat. Blend in sugar and then egg. Sift together flour, baking powder, and salt and stir in. Add vanilla, nuts. Spread in well-greased and floured 8-by-8-by-2-inch pan. Bake 20-25 minutes. While warm, cut into squares.

–Dr. Helen Falls

¼ c. butter
1 egg
1 t. baking powder
½ t. vanilla
½ c. chopped nuts
1 c. light brown sugar, packed
¾ c. sifted flour
½ t. salt

CHOCO-CHEWY SCOTCH BARS (Serves 12)

In the top of a double boiler, melt chocolate, milk, and 2 tablespoons butter and blend until smooth. Combine 1 cup butter, sugar, and eggs; add flour and salt and blend. Stir in vanilla, nuts, and coconut. Mix well. Put in jellyroll pan. Marble with chocolate. Bake in 350° oven, 30-35 minutes.

–Mrs. Bob Neil (Julia)

1 (12 oz.) pkg. chocolate bits
2 T. butter
1 box brown sugar
2 c. flour
1 t. vanilla
½ c. coconut
1 (15 oz.) can sweetened condensed milk
1 c. butter, melted
2 eggs
1 T. salt
½ c. nuts

CATHEDRAL COOKIES (Makes 60)

1 stick margarine
1 (12 oz.) pkg. chocolate chips
2 eggs
confectioner's sugar
1 pkg. miniature marshmallows, colored
2 c. pecans, chopped and toasted

In double boiler, melt margarine and chocolate chips. Stir in beaten eggs and cook until thick. Set aside to cool. When mixture has cooled enough to melt marshmallows, add marshmallows and nuts. On 4 (12-inch) pieces of waxed paper, sprinkle confectioner's sugar. Divide chocolate mixture into 4 portions and roll in wax paper. Freeze. When ready to serve, slice thin with sharp knife.

–Mrs. Chester Vaughn (Evelyn)

CHOCOLATE MINT STICKS (Serves 12-15)

2 sq. unsweetened chocolate
½ c. margarine
2 eggs
1 c. sugar
½ t. peppermint extract
1 T. corn syrup
½ c. all-purpose flour, sifted
dash salt
½ c. nuts, chopped

Melt chocolate and margarine over hot water. Blend eggs and sugar thoroughly. Add chocolate mixture to egg mixture; then add other ingredients. Pour into well-greased 9-inch square pan. Bake at 325° for 25 minutes. Cool. Spread filling on top.

Filling:

2 T. margarine
1 cup confectioner's sugar
1 T. milk
¾ t. peppermint extract

Work margarine and sugar together. Add other ingredients. Spread over baked mixture and refrigerate while preparing glaze.

Glaze:

2 sq. semi-sweet chocolate
¼ t. vanilla
2 T. margarine

Melt over hot water. Stir thoroughly and dribble over cooled filling. Tilt back and forth until glaze covers surface. Refrigerate about 30 minutes. Cut into thin strips.

–Mrs. Chester Vaughn (Evelyn)

PEPPERMINT FRUIT ROLL (Serves 8)

1 c. White Lily self-rising flour
3 heaping T. shortening (Crisco)
½ c. buttermilk
1 c. sugar
1 can diluted frozen orange juice (dilute according to directions)

Cut shortening and flour together; add milk with spoon until a *stiff* consistency; knead thoroughly on wax paper; roll thin; cut in 7-inch squares. (NOTE: You may substitute your own recipe for pie crust if you like.) In center of each square, put 2 tablespoons fruit (pared and cut in small pieces); add one heaping tablespoon sugar; 1 stick candy (crushed in paper it comes in); thick slice of butter. Pull ends of pastry together; turn over and place in pan (deeper pan than rolls); leave ¼-inch between each roll. On top of each roll place on tablespoon sugar, heavy slice of butter. Press half stick candy on very top. Pour orange juice in pan until rolls are about two-thirds covered. Bake in preheated 450° oven until brown.

–Mrs. George Herndon (Claire)

2 or 3 ripe apples
12 small sticks peppermint candy
1 stick margarine

Prize-winning recipe by the late Dr. Willey D. Ogletree, beloved pastor of churches in Alabama for over 50 years. Dr. Ogletree won first prize (a new car) in a national contest sponsored by White Lily Flour for this original recipe when he was about 78 years old. He prepared the dish on local television in Montgomery, Alabama, and gave his Christian witness at the same time.

PEANUT BUTTER COOKIES (Makes dozen)

Mix above ingredients. Make into balls and flatten with a fork. Bake at 350° until done.

–Mrs. George Flanagan (Brenda)

1 c. sugar
1 egg
1 c. crunchy peanut butter

CHINESE ALMOND COOKIES

Sift into a large bowl, flour, sugar, salt, and baking powder. Using pastry blender, cut in butter until mixture resembles coarse corn meal. Beat egg with 2 tablespoons water and the almond extract. Add to flour mixture, mixing with fork until dough leaves sides of bowl. On lightly floured surface, knead dough until smooth. Wrap in wax paper; refrigerate 1 hour.

2½ c. sifted flour
¾ c. sugar
¼ t. salt
1 t. baking powder
¾ c. butter
1 egg
1 t. almond extract
about 36 whole blanched almonds
1 egg yolk

Meanwhile, preheat oven to 350°. Form dough into balls 1 inch in diameter. Place 3 inches apart on an ungreased cookie sheet. With palm of hand, flatten each cookie to a circle ¼-inch thick; press almond into center of each. Combine egg yolk with 1 tablespoon water; brush on cookies. Bake 20-25 minutes or until golden brown.

–Mrs. Grady Cothen (Bettye)

CHOCOLATE COOKIES

½ c. butter or margarine
1 egg
2½ c. flour
½ t. salt
vanilla
1 c. sugar
2 sq. baking chocolate
2 t. baking powder
2 T. milk

Cream butter; add other ingredients. Chill. Roll thin and cut. Bake at 350° until golden brown.

–Dr. Helen Falls

CONGO BARS

1 lb. brown sugar
2 eggs
1 (6 oz.) pkg. carbo chips (found in health food stores)
1 t. vanilla
2 c. unbleached flour (or 1 c. unbleached and 1 c. whole wheat)
1 c. oil (preferabley peanut)
2 t. baking powder
2 T. milk
⅔ c. pecans

Mix all together and bake at 350° for 30-45 minutes. Do not overcook. They are supposed to be very chewy.

–Mrs. Jerry Garrard (Ruthie)

COOK-WHILE-YOU-SLEEP-COOKIES (Makes 40-50)

2 egg whites
pinch of salt
¼ t. cream of tartar
⅔ c. sugar
¼ t. vanilla
1 c. chopped nuts
1 c. chocolate morsels

Preheat oven to 350°. Beat egg whites until foamy; add salt and cream of tartar and beat until stiff. Add sugar, 2 tablespoons at a time, beating well after each addition. Stir in vanilla, nuts, and chocolate.

Drop by teaspoonfuls onto cookie sheets

lined with aluminum foil. Put in oven and turn off heat immediately. Do not open oven door for at least 8 hours. Carefully remove cookies from foil.

–Dr. Helen Falls

SISTER'S COOKIES (Makes 12 dozen)

½ lb. margarine
1 c. white sugar
1 c. brown sugar
2 eggs
2 c. all-purpose flour
½ t. salt
1 t. soda
1 t. baking powder
2 c. oatmeal
1 c. coconut
1 c. chopped nuts
1 t. vanilla

Cream shortening; add sugar gradually, beating well after each addition. Add eggs and beat well. Add flour, salt, soda, and baking powder that have been sifted together. Add the other ingredients in order given. Mix well and drop by teaspoonfuls on greased cookie sheet. Bake in 350° oven for about 8 minutes or until light brown.

–Mrs. Hugh Tobias (Marie Rush)

HAYSTACKS (Makes 30 pieces)

1 (6 oz.) pkg. butterscotch morsels
1 (3 oz.) can chow mein noodles
2 t. salad oil
2 c. miniature marshmallows

In double boiler over hot, *not boiling,* water, melt butterscotch morsels. Stir in salad oil. In large bowl, mix chow mein noodles and marshmallows; pour on butterscotch and mix thoroughly with fork. On wax-paper-lined cookie sheet, drop mixture by heaping teaspoonfuls. (If mixture thickens, place over hot water a few minutes.) Chill until set.

–Dr. Helen Falls

M & M COOKIES (Makes 6 dozen)

2 sticks margarine
½ c. granulated sugar
2 t. vanilla
1 t. salt
1½ c. M &Ms
1 c. brown sugar
2 eggs
1 t. baking soda
2¼ c. flour

Cream shortening, sugars, eggs, and vanilla. Sift flour, soda, and salt. Add dry ingredients to creamed mixture and mix well. Add half the M & M candies and save rest to decorate the tops. Drop by teaspoonfuls on baking sheet and bake at 375° for 10-12 minutes.

–Dr. Helen Falls

DUTCH HAIL (Makes 30 bars)

Preheat oven (350°). Lightly grease a jellyroll pan (15½-by-10½-by-1 inch). Mix butter, sugar, and egg yolk. Blend flour and cinnamon; stir into butter mixture. Pat into pan. Beat water and egg white until frothy. Brush over dough and sprinkle with nuts. Bake 30-35 minutes or until very light brown. Cut immediately into fingerlike strips. *–Jan Hagel*
Mrs. Paul Gericke (Jean)

1 c. (2 sticks) butter
1 c. sugar
1 egg, separated
2¼ c. flour
½ t. cinnamon
1 T. water
½ c. very finely chopped walnuts

TRAVIS HOUSE COOKIES

Add brown sugar to egg white; stir in flour, salt, then pecans. Drop by small spoonfuls (far apart) on buttered cookie sheet. Bake at 325° for 10 minutes. Remove when partly cooled. *–Mrs. J. C. Hamilton (Barbara)*

1 egg white, beaten to stiff froth
1 c. brown sugar (packed)
1 T. flour (level)
pinch of salt
1 c. chopped pecans

ROLLED DATE COOKIES

Cream sugars, shortening, and oleo; add beaten eggs and mix. Sift remaining ingredients together. Add dry ingredients and mix. Dough will be stiff. Roll out (divide into 4 parts) to ½-inch thickness on lightly floured surface. Spread date mixture on dough. Roll up. Let stand in refrigerator overnight. Slice and bake in 350° oven. NOTE: May be frozen.

1 c. white sugar
1 c. brown sugar
3 eggs, beaten
½ c. shortening
½ c. oleo
4 c. flour
1 t. soda
1 t. salt
1 t. vanilla

Filling:

Cook first three ingredients until thickened. Add nuts. Cool before spreading on cookie dough. *–Mrs. John McPherson (Marie)*

2 lb. dates, cut fine
½ c. sugar
¾ c. water
½ c. chopped nuts

SEVEN-LAYER BARS

Melt butter in 13-by-9-by-2-inch baking pan. Sprinkle crumbs evenly over butter. Sprinkle on coconut, chocolate and but-

¼ c. butter or margarine
1 c. graham cracker crumbs
1 c. shredded coconut
1 (6 oz.) pkg. semi-sweet

terscotch pieces. Pour sweetened condensed milk evenly over top. Sprinkle on nuts. Press lightly into pan. Bake in moderate oven (350°) for 30 minutes. Cut into bars while still slightly warm.

–Mrs. Thomas Cobb (Lillie)
Mrs. Wayne Hoggle (Romie)
Mrs. Cecil Braselli (Candy)

chocolate chips
1 (6 oz.) pkg. butterscotch pieces
1 (15 oz.) can sweetened condensed milk
1 c. chopped nuts

POLKA DOT COOKIES (Makes 4 dozen)

Cream margarine and sugars. Blend in egg and vanilla. Sift together flour, baking powder, salt, and soda; add alternately with milk, mixing well after each addition. Stir in chocolate pieces, cherries, and nuts. Place rounded teaspoonfuls of dough on greased baking sheets. Bake at 375° for 10-12 minutes.

–Mrs. Bob Neil (Judy)

½ c. margarine
½ c. granulated sugar
½ c. brown sugar, packed
1 egg, beaten
1 t. vanilla
2 c. flour
1 t. baking powder
½ t. salt
¼ t. baking soda
¼ c. milk
1 (6 oz.) pkg. semi-sweet chocolate bits
½ c. chopped maraschino cherries
½ c. chopped pecans

OATMEAL CRUNCHY BAR (Serves 6)

Melt butter, sugar, and syrup in pan. Add oats and salt; mix well. Spread in pan 8-by-12 inches and bake in moderate oven for 15-20 minutes or until golden brown and firm to touch. Cut in squares or fingers while warm. Cool in tin, then remove carefully. A nutritious treat for children after school.

–Mrs. Fisher Humphreys

4 oz. butter
1 T. brown sugar
4 T. Karo syrup
8 oz. rolled oats (a little over 1¼ c.)
pinch of salt

OATMEAL COOKIES

Put shortening, sugar, egg, water, and vanilla in a bowl and beat vigorously. Sift dry ingredients and add to shortening mixture. Mix well. Blend in oats and wheat germ. Drop by teaspoonfuls on greased cookie sheet. Bake at 350° for 12-15 minutes. If desired, add nuts, raisins, dates, coconut, or

¾ c. shortening
1½ c. brown sugar, packed
1 egg
¼ c. water
1 t. vanilla
1 c. sifted flour
½ c. dry milk
½ t. soda
1 t. salt

chocolate chips. You can substitute Wheatena Cereal for the wheat germ and you may use ¼ cup whole wheat flour and ¾ cup regular flour in place of all white flour if desired. *–Mrs. Ray Davidson (Virginia)*

2 c. rolled oats, uncooked
1 c. wheat germ

OATMEAL LACE COOKIES (Makes 11 dozen)

Mix all ingredients. Drop by level teaspoonfuls on well-buttered cookie sheet. Bake in moderate (375°) oven about 4 minutes, watching closely. Let cool a moment before removing from cookie sheet.

–Mrs. Claude Howe (Joyce)

2¼ c. quick-cooking rolled oats
2¼ c. packed light brown sugar
1 t. salt
1 t. vanilla
3 T. flour
1 c. butter, melted
1 egg, slightly beaten

GRANDMOTHER'S OATMEAL COOKIES (Makes 6 dozen)

Combine eggs, raisins, and vanilla. Let mixture stand 1 hour. Thoroughly cream shortening and sugars. Sift flour, salt, soda, and cinnamon into sugar mixture. Mix well. Blend in eggs, raisins, oatmeal, and nuts. (Dough will be stiff.) Drop dough by heaping teaspoonfulls onto greased cookie sheet. Bake in a preheated 350° oven for 10-12 minutes until light brown.

–Mrs. J. Hardee Kennedy (Virginia)

3 eggs
1 c. raisins
1 t. vanilla
1 c. shortening
1 c. brown sugar
½ c. chopped nuts
2½ c. sifted flour
1 t. salt
1 t. soda
1 t. cinnamon
2 c. oatmeal
1 c. white sugar

PRALINE CANDY (Serves 16)

Cook all ingredients except pecans on medium heat, stirring frequently. At soft-ball stage, remove from heat and whip with spoon for 1 minute. Stir in pecans and drop by spoonfuls onto buttered tray.

–Margaret Stewart

2 c. granulated sugar
2 T. butter
pinch of salt
1 c. buttermilk
1 t. baking soda
⅔ c. chopped pecans

AFTER-DINNER MINTS

Mix sugar, water, and syrup in boiler. Cook to hard-ball stage. Remove from heat and add cream of tartar. Pour cooked syrup over

2 c. sugar
¼ t. cream of tartar
food coloring
2-3 drops peppermint flavoring

stiffly beaten egg white. Add flavoring and coloring. Beat for five minutes. Roll into long narrow strips and cut into small pillows with scissors. *–Mrs. Dan Ireland (Polly)*

½ c. water
1 egg white, beaten stiff
½ c. white corn syrup

PEANUT BLOSSOMS (Makes 48)

Combine all ingredients except candy in large mixing bowl. Mix on lowest speed of mixer until dough forms. Shape dough into 48 balls. Roll balls in sugar and place on ungreased cookie sheet. Bake at 375° for 9-10 minutes. Top each cookie immediately with a candy kiss. Press down firmly until cookie cracks. *–Mrs. Dan Ireland (Polly)*

1¾ c. flour
½ c. sugar
½ c. shortening
2 T. milk
1 t. soda
½ c. firmly packed brown sugar
½ c. peanut butter
1 t. vanilla
½ t. salt
1 egg
48 chocolate kisses

MARGARET'S NEVER-FAIL PEANUT BRITTLE

Grease 2 cookie sheets. Place sugar, Karo, and water in heavy boiler (I use my pressure cooker 4-quart boiler). Cook to 230°. Then add raw peanuts. Cook, stirring often, until temperature reaches 300°. Remove from heat and add butter, soda, and vanilla. Stir well. Quickly pour onto greased cookie sheets, spreading as thin as possible. When done, break into pieces.

–Mrs. John F. Gibson

(For best results, always use candy thermometer)
2 c. sugar
1 c. white Karo
½ c. water
2-3 c. raw peanuts
2 T. butter
1 t. soda
1½ t. vanilla flavoring

STRAWBERRIES (Serves 30)

Mix all ingredients together in bowl. Take small amount of mixture and form into the shape of strawberries. Dip the flat end in granulated sugar that has been colored green and dip the pointed end in sugar that has been colored red. Insert green toothpicks or colored pieces of nut into the strawberry to look like a stem.

–Mrs. Elmo McLaurin (Sandra)

2 pkg. strawberry jello
¾ c. sweetened condensed milk
green and red food coloring
1 c. flaked coconut
1 c. finely chopped pecans
toothpicks

Metric Equivalents

Milk	1 liter	1.06 quarts
Butter	1 kilogram	2.2 pounds
Lemon juice	1 gram	0.035 ounces
Flour	1 liter	4.23 cups
Sugar	1 milliliter	0.067 tablespoons
Salt	1 milliliter	0.203 teaspoons
Water	1 liter	2.1 pints

1 cup = 250 milliliters (ml.)
¼ cup = 62½ milliliters
1 teaspoon = 5 milliliters
1 tablespoon = 15 milliliters
1 pint = 0.47 liter (l.)

1 quart = 0.95 liter
1 gallon = 3.81 liter
1 liter = 2.1 pint
1 liter = 1.06 quart
1 liter = 0.26 gallon

APPENDIX I

Dispensing Southern Hospitality

Hospitality, a synonym for the South, comes from the heart. Hospitality is a gift: it is the giving of oneself, the opening of one's home to create a warm and welcoming spot where friends or strangers may be completely at their ease. If a guest takes his leave feeling that he has brought joy to his host and happiness to the household, then he has received hospitality.

How to Plan a Party

1. Decide on the kind of party, the guest list for the party, and the date, and send or telephone invitations two weeks before that date.

2. Keep in mind standard meal schedules and party times in planning your gathering. Take into consideration, also, the customs of your community. Here are some general guidelines:

Brunch: Between 10:30 A.M. and 1:00 P.M.
Luncheon: Begins at 12:30 or 1:00 P.M. and lasts 1½-2 hours.
Buffet luncheon: Begins at 12:30 P.M. and lasts until 2:00 P.M.
Dinner: Metropolitan areas, 8:00 P.M.; smaller communities, between 6:30 and 7:00 P.M.
Buffet suppers: Begins 7:30 or 8:00 P.M.
Morning coffee: Between 10:00 A.M. and noon.
Tea party: From 4:00 P.M. (not later than 4:30) to 5:00 or 5:30 P.M.

3. Write out your menu. Buy staple items one week ahead (spread out the cost this way); but the rest of the food no later than the day before the party. If possible, cook and freeze several items ahead of time.

4. List those dishes that may be prepared ahead of time, and note how *far* ahead this may be done. List even the separate steps in preparing food that, though minor, are pure nuisance: toasting bread crumbs, chopping nuts, mincing parsley.

5. Make two schedules: (1) a daily order of battle made simultaneously with selection of the menu and (2) an hourly plan written down early on the day of the party.

6. Make a countdown. Specify in writing the exact time appetizers need to be removed from the refrigerator or freezer; decide when to drain the celery sticks and when to plug in the coffee pot.

7. Do your heavy cleaning as much ahead of time as possible. Check your crystal, silver, china, and linen to be sure they are all ready.

8. Collect the items you need for your centerpiece at least the day before.

9. Do miscellaneous errands the day *before* the party.

10. Decide what you're going to wear to the party, and be sure it is ready for you to step into. Be sure to leave ample time to dress before the guests arrive.

11. Set the table the night before the party. If you're having many guests and many tables, number the tables. When guests arrive, have them draw numbers for their tables.

12. Party day: (a) Do centerpiece, (b) finish cooking, (c) straighten house, and (d) clean guest bath.

13. Turn on your front porch lights or floodlights at least forty-five minutes before party time if yours is an evening party.

14. Relax and enjoy yourself.

Special Touches

1. Do something unusual. Plan to decorate your house and table according to the mood you want to create for a party. Even a flickering candle in the entryway can softly announce a warm welcome.

2. Candles always look lovely on a table, but don't plan to use them unless you also plan to light them. Light candles only after sundown, when the lights dim outside, or on a dark, gloomy day. Never use candles (not even in a decorative arrangement) that do not have charred wicks. Light them first, then blow out quickly.

3. A large pot of flowers on the front step is a very festive way to say welcome to your guests. Try one outside your door or in the entry hall next time you entertain.

4. In the Old South, the pineapple, greatly loved by all, was carved above the door of homes as a symbol of hospitality. A fruit bowl of bite-sized chunks of fully ripened fresh pineapple is beautiful combined with vivid strawberries. Provide your guests with toothpicks for picking up the fruit and with bowls of sugar for dipping it. Set out brown sugar for the pineapple and powdered sugar for the strawberries.

5. In the spring, buy potted geraniums to use in a basket for a centerpiece; later, put the geraniums out in the garden. Your enjoyment of the flowers will be double.

6. In the fall, have ready one or two arrangements of dried flowers to use as table decorations. A favorite autumn centerpiece is bright red apples in a Paul Revere bowl, a simple but beautiful statement.

7. Call on the natural grace of an ivy leaf to complement both a casual and elegant table setting. To make ivy place cards, choose undamaged, medium-to-large-sized leaves, and rinse them to clean away outdoor dust. Dry the leaves thoroughly, then, with opaque white ink and an inexpensive stylus and pen, write each guest's name right on the leaf. To repeat the ivy theme, use trailing stems for a centerpiece either alone or in combination with an arrangement of flowers. Tie a small bow, if you wish, on the stems of each ivy place card. Decorating with ivy is particularly convenient because it is available all year round.

8. An interesting tea table is enhanced by serving cookies and sandwiches on plates of various heights—some flat, some stemmed, some fluted, and some tiered. Use paper doilies (never plastic) on all the serving trays you plan to use (whether silver, china, or crystal) except for a ceramic platter for raw vegetables.

9. A variety of sandwich cutters for preparing sandwiches is a great asset, as sandwiches cut in fancy shapes add interest to any occasion. Cut bread slices ahead of time and store (covered with barely damp paper towels) in a closed container in the refrigerator until ready to use.

10. An artistically arranged fruit platter may serve as the centerpiece for a buffet, as well as make a delicious salad. For color, combine strawberries, watermelon balls, or maraschino cherries with canned and seasonal fruits. The platter may be arranged ahead of time, covered with plastic wrap, and refrigerated. For fruits that discolor, remember to first sprinkle on lemon juice or acidic dressing. Dip banana slices in lemon juice and sprinkle with flaked coconut.

11. Make citrus cups by cutting oranges in half, scooping out the slices with a grapefruit knife, and then making sawtoothed edges. First cut slashes in all one direction in orange shell; then cut in the other direction. Fill shells with chilled fresh fruit and and garnish with mint leaves.

12. Lemon cups filled with tartar sauce make an eye-appealing border for seafood.

13. An attractive way to serve chicken salad would be to place it in the center of cantaloupe or honey dew melon rings placed on a bed of lettuce.

14. Don't forget the decorative qualities of an ice ring when planning your table settings. See "Beverages," p. 17 for instructions on how to create a colorful mold of fruit slices, flowers, and mint.

APPENDIX II

Helpful Hints

For quick and *handy seasoning* while cooking, keep on hand a large shaker containing 6 parts salt and 1 part pepper.

It is important when and *how you add salt in cooking.* To blend with soups and sauces, put it in early, but add it to meats just before taking it from the stove. In cake ingredients, salt can be mixed with the eggs.

Soak *bacon* in cold water for a few minutes before placing in a skillet to cook. This will lessen the tendency to shrink and curl.

Fry several pounds of bacon at one time. *Store bacon in the freezer*. Just take out the number of slices you need, run under the boiler for just a minute, and they will taste like fried. This saves spattering up your stove every time you want bacon. It also saves time during the morning rush.

Crying in the onions? Peel onion and put in freezer for about 10 minutes before chopping.

If you do not have a transparent *double boiler* (sometimes all the water will boil out and the pan will scorch), just place a few marbles in the bottom when you start to cook. When the water begins to dry up, the marbles will dance and notify you.

A leaf of lettuce dropped into the pot absorbs the grease from the top of soup. Remove the lettuce and throw away.

Add a little vinegar to the water *when an egg cracks during boiling.* It will help to seal the egg.

Add a tablespoon of fat to *cooking water for spaghetti* to keep the water from boiling over.

If *a cracked dish* is boiled for 45 minutes in sweet milk, the crack will be so welded together that it will be hardly visible. Moreover, it will be strong enough to stand the same use as before.

Use the type of can opener that leaves a smooth edge on a can; remove both ends from a tuna-fish size can, and you have a perfect mold for *poaching eggs*.

Keep a dishpan of soapy water in the sink while you're fixing dinner. Drop in each used utensil for an early soaking and *easy cleanup*.

Fill *burned pots* and pans with a solution of baking soda, 1 teaspoon in a quart of hot water. Leave in pan until cooled and cleaning will be greatly simplified.

To remove burned food from the oven, place a small cloth saturated with ammonia inside overnight and food will wipe away easily the next morning.

Wash hands with salt *to remove odors* such as garlic, onion, cleanser, and so forth.

Chocolate stains on clothing may be removed with a paste of borax and water.

If you break an *egg on the floor*, sprinkle it heavily with Salt and leave it alone for 5-10 minutes. Sweep the dried egg into a dust pan.

Cleaning solution for tile: Mix 1 cup detergent, 1 gallon water, and 1 cup bleach, allow to stand on tile for one hour, and rinse off. Let the tile dry; rub lemon oil over the surface; let it dry again.

Food to Serve 100

To serve 50 people, divide by 2;
to serve 25 people, divide by 4.

Coffee	3 pounds
Cream	3 quarts
Milk	6 gallons
Fruit Juice	4 (6½-7 lb. 5 oz.) cans
Soup	5 gallons
Weiners	25 pounds
Ham	40 pounds
Roast Pork	40 pounds
Chicken for Chicken Pie	40 pounds
Scalloped Potatoes	5 gallons
Baked Beans	5 gallons
Cauliflower	18 pounds
Carrots	33 pounds
Rolls	200
Potato Salad	12 quarts
Lettuce	20 heads
Pies	18
Loaf Sugar	3 pounds
Whipping Cream	4 pints
Fruit Cocktail	2½ gallons
Tomato Juice	4 (6½-7 lb. 5 oz.) cans
Oysters	18 quarts
Meat Loaf	24 pounds
Beef	40 pounds
Hamburger	30-36 pounds
Potatoes	35 pounds
Vegetables	4 (6½-7 lb. 5 oz.) cans
Beets	30 pounds
Cabbage for slaw	20 pounds
Bread	10 loaves
Butter	3 pounds

Fruit Salad	20 quarts
Salad Dressing	3 quarts
Ice Cream	4 gallons
Cheese	3 pounds
Pickles	2 quarts
Olives	1¾ pounds
Nuts	3 pounds

Weights and Measures

3 teaspoons = 1 tablespoon
4 tablespoons = ½ cup
5⅓ tablespoons = ⅓ cup
8 tablespoons = ½ cup
12 tablespoons = ¾ cup
10⅔ tablespoons = ⅔ cup
16 tablespoons = 1 cup
½ cup = 1 gill
2 cups = 1 pint

4 cups =1 quart
4 quarts =1 gallon
8 quarts =1 peck
4 pecks = 1 bushel
32 ounces = 1 quart
16 ounces =1 pound
8 ounces liquid =1 cup
1 ounce liquid = 2 tablespoons

Equivalents and Substitutions

Equivalents

American cheese	1 pound = 2⅔ cups cubed
Baking powder	1 cup = 5½ ounces
Cocoa	1 pound = 4 cups ground
Coffee	1 pound = 5 cups ground
Cornmeal	1 pound = 3 cups
Cornstarch	1 pound = 3 cups
Cracker crumbs	23 soda crackers = 1 cup
Graham crackers	15 crackers = 1 cup
Eggs	1 egg = 5 tablespoons liquid
	4-5 eggs = 1 cup
	7-9 whites = 1 cup
	12-14 yolks = 1 cup
Flour	1 pound all-purpose = 4 cups
	1 pound cake = 4½ cups
	1 pound graham = 3½ cups
Lemons, juice	1 medium lemon = 2-3 tablespoons
	5-8 medium lemons = 1 cup juice
Lemons, rind	1 lemon grated = 1 tablespoon rind
Oranges	1 medium orange = 2-3 tablespoons juice
	3-4 medium oranges =1 cup juice
Gelatin	3¼ ounce package flavored = ½ cup
	¼ ounce package unflavored = 1 tablespoon
Shortening or butter	1 pound = 2 cups

Sugar ------------------------	1 pound brown = 2½ cups 1 pound cube =96-100 cubes 1 pound granulated = 2 cups 1 pound powdered = 3½ cups

Substitutions

Ingredient called for:	*Substitution*
1 cup self-rising flour	1 cup all-purpose flour plus 1 t. baking powder and ½ t. salt
1 cup cake flour	1 cup all-purpose flour minus 2 T.
1 t. baking powder	½ t. cream of tartar plus ¼ t. soda
1 T. cornstarch or arrowroot	2 T. all-purpose flour
1 T. tapioca	1½ T. all-purpose flour
1 whole egg	2 egg yolks plus 1 T. water
1 cup commercial sour cream	1 T. lemon juice plus evaporated milk to equal 1 cup, 3 T. butter plus ⅞ cup of sour milk
1 cup yoghurt	1 cup buttermilk or sour milk
1 cup sour milk or buttermilk	1 T. vinegar or lemon juice plus sweet milk to equal 1 cup
1 cup honey	1¼ cups sugar plus ¼ cup liquid
1 ounce unsweetened chocolate	3 T. cocoa plus 1 T. butter
1 clove fresh garlic	1 t. garlic salt or ⅛ t. garlic powder
1 t. onion powder	2 t. minced onion
1 T. fresh herbs	1 t. ground or crushed dry herbs
1 pound fresh mushrooms	6 ounces canned mushrooms
1 cup butter or oleo	⅞ cup lard with ½ teaspoon salt or 1 cup hydrogenated fat (oil) plus ½ teaspoon salt
1 cup whole milk	½ cup evaporated milk plus ½ cup water. Or 4 tablespoons dry whole milk plus 1 cup of water, or 4 tablespoons nonfat dry milk plus 2 teaspoons fat and 1 cup water
1 cup skim milk	4 tablespoons nonfat dry milk plus 1 cup water
1 tablespoon flour for thickening	½ tablespoon cornstarch, potato starch or arrowroot starch or 1 tablespoon tapioca
1 cup all-purpose flour	½ cup bran, whole wheat flour or corn meal plus enough of all-purpose flour to fill cup

Index